A Mystical Portrait of Jesus

New Perspectives on John's Gospel

Demetrius R. Dumm, O.S.B.

THE LITURGICAL PRESS
Collegeville, Minnesota

www.litpress.org

I gratefully acknowledge the encouragement and generous financial support of my former student, Bishop Nicholas Dattilo of the Diocese of Harrisburg. I have also benefited greatly from the encouragement of my abbot, Douglas Nowicki, O.S.B. and from the insights and suggestions of my confrere Campion Gavaler O.S.B. Finally, I must recognize the constant and cheerful assistance of our faculty secretary, Nancy Ravis.

Cover design by David Manahan, O.S.B. Illustration: Georges Rouault, French, 1871–1958. *The Head of Christ*, 1938. Oil on canvas, 104.8 x 74.9 cm. © The Cleveland Museum of Art, 2001. Purchase from the Hanna Fund, 1950.399.

1   2   3   4   5   6   7   8

Library of Congress Cataloging-in-Publication Data

Dumm, Demetrius, 1923–
    A mystical portrait of Jesus : new perspectives on John's Gospel / Demetrius R. Dumm.
        p. cm.
    Includes bibliographical references and index.
    ISBN 0-8146-2760-9 (alk. paper)
    1. Bible. N.T. John—Criticism, interpretation, etc. I. Title.

BS2615.2 .D855 2001
226.5'06—dc21

                                                      2001033168

I dedicate this book to all my teachers.

In particular, I remember with special gratitude Rosaline Kirkpatrick, who instilled in me a love of learning in the unlikely setting of a one-room country elementary school. During my seminary years at St. Vincent, I was enthralled by the philosophical insights of Oliver Grosselin, O.S.B. and by the enthusiasm of my Scripture professor, Justin Krellner, O.S.B. By far the most influential professor at Sant' Anselmo in Rome was Cipriano Vagaggini, O.S.B. Finally, at the École Biblique in Jerusalem, I fell under the spell of Roland DeVaux, O.P. and Pierre Benoit, O.P. To all of these great teachers I owe an eternal debt of gratitude.

Contents

Introduction

Anyone who has visited the biblical section of a library must wonder whether we really need another book on John's Gospel. Literature about this Gospel is voluminous and there is no sign that the flow will decrease any time soon. Nonetheless, this literature is so dominated by scientific analysis that it seems worthwhile to offer a book that benefits from such scientific study but which seeks to discover the deeper, spiritual meaning in this Gospel. Great strides have in fact been made in recent years toward an interpretation of the Bible that respects scientific interpretation but strives to go beyond that to plumb the depths of a faith-guided understanding. Such an endeavor is especially appropriate in the case of John's Gospel, which is so sensitive to the spiritual, symbolic dimension of biblical revelation.

Another Look at Biblical Interpretation

Since John's Gospel is so obviously intent on expressing the spiritual implications of the words and deeds of Jesus, it is probably the clearest example of the basic inadequacy of the historical-critical method *alone* in the quest for the fullest and richest meaning of Scripture. This does not at all imply that the historical-critical method is optional for a biblical scholar, and the 1993 Instruction of the Pontifical Biblical Commission makes this clear in its statement that "the historical-critical method is the indispensable method for the scientific study of the meaning of ancient texts" (*The Interpretation of the Bible in the Church*, 5). However, the same Instruction is quick to add: "For all its overall validity, the historical-critical method cannot claim to be totally sufficient for comprehending the biblical texts in all their richness" (Ibid., 7).

The problem is, of course, that the Gospel of John, while written in human language, claims to convey divine truth. After all, it is this Gospel which tells us that "the Word was with God" (1:1) and then "became flesh and lived among us" (1:14), so that the message heard in heaven might be brought to us here on earth. However, since human words cannot bear the full weight of divine meaning, the classic solution has been to employ symbolism, which gives wings, as it were, to human words so that they might carry the weight of transcendent and divine meaning.

In this way, not only human words, but also human persons and events, while remaining literal or historical, can be wonderfully enhanced by an added symbolic meaning. They become "larger than life" as they take on a universal and perennial meaning over and above their particular and time-bound significance. Thus, for example, when Jesus meets a Samaritan woman at Jacob's well, it is not just an interesting episode of ancient history. Rather, the "living water" which he offers her becomes an invitation to all subsequent hearers to abandon the stale well water of a purely natural existence and to accept Jesus' offer of fresh, living water which is the vibrant, exciting life of faith.

An awareness of symbolic meaning gives perennial significance to the lives of historical people in the Bible also. Thus, King David and King Saul were historical kings of Israel, but their stories convey rich symbolic meaning as well. King David's faith and confidence and success, in spite of personal tragedies, become a model for all believers, just as the doubt and timidity and suicide of his counterpart, King Saul, is a warning to all believers. In a sense, both confident David and fearful Saul exist in all of us. The text then challenges us to appropriate the confident faith of David and to reject the dark, brooding attitude of Saul. Symbolic interpretation thus makes their stories significant for our present world.

Unfortunately, there is a tendency in our technologically dominated society to limit truth to what is "factual," so that what is symbolic is judged to be untrue. As a matter of fact, however, when it comes to spiritual or divine truth, only symbolism is able to express it adequately, so that this most important of all truths is often conveyed in a "non-factual" manner! Sandra Schneiders makes this crystal clear when she writes: "We are increasingly aware today that fact and truth are not identical and that often enough the truth is best conveyed by the non-literal, for example, by symbol, myth or story" (*Written That You May Believe,* 64). This is, of course, especially true when we are dealing with transcendent or divine truth.

Schneiders provides an excellent definition of symbol as it is used in biblical literature and particularly in John's Gospel: It is "(1) a sensible reality (2) which renders present to and (3) involves a person subjectively in (4) a *transforming experience* (5) of *transcendent mystery*" (*Written That You May Believe,* 66, emphasis added). We note immediately that symbolic language is most appropriate for biblical revelation which is intended to bring about conversion ("transforming experience") and to put us in touch with divine power ("transcendent mystery").

This also explains why purely scientific interpretation has serious problems when it attempts to deal with the highly symbolic nature of John's Gospel. Schneiders writes:

> No matter how slippery such terrain (of gospel interpretation) originally appeared to be to scholars trained in a highly positivistic historical-critical type of exegesis, it became necessary to reengage the issue of symbolism in the Gospel of John. If a text is intrinsically symbolic, there is no such thing as a valid, purely "literal" interpretation of it. Non-symbolic interpretation of a

symbolic text is not literal; it is inadequate (*Written That You May Believe*, 65).

Thus, symbolic interpretation is not something grudgingly accepted as a last resort; it is the first and only adequate interpretation of most Johannine texts.

In order to appreciate this symbolic dimension, one must be attuned to the transcendent world and that can happen only through the charism of faith. We know, of course, that the insights of faith cannot be fully verified scientifically. However, they are not at all incompatible with valid scientific conclusions. The world of science and the world of the Bible are different worlds, but they need not be contradictory. In the case of the Bible, scientific interpretation provides a solid basis, but it is not the end of the process. When faith is authentic, and not just some strongly held opinion, it provides access to a rich meaning of Scripture which cannot be discovered by any other means.

It should be obvious, therefore, that the charism of faith, which attunes us to the reality of the divine or transcendent world, will be necessary if one wishes to plumb the depths of Johannine revelation. But this faith must be more than the acceptance of certain true statements about God. It must be a personal discovery of the reality of a larger world within which this world and one's own life take on a whole new meaning and purpose. In this way, the believer is put in touch with *all* reality and not just the relatively ephemeral reality of daily existence.

The Uniqueness of John's Gospel

Even a cursory comparison of the Fourth Gospel with the Synoptic Gospels will highlight its uniqueness. For instance, in John's Gospel, Jesus is the eternal Word who became flesh so that he might bring us the truth about his heavenly Father. Accordingly, the divinity of Jesus is on display everywhere. There is no need of a transfiguration, and there is only a passing reference to the agony in the garden. There is a Last Supper but, amazingly, there is no institution of the Eucharist there, whereas a long treatment of the Eucharist occurs in chapter 6. In John's Gospel, Jesus centers his activity in Judea rather than Galilee. In the passion story itself, where John's Gospel is most similar to the Synoptics, there is a detailed account of the trial before Pilate, while the trial before the high priest is scarcely mentioned. Finally, much attention is given to the anonymous "disciple whom Jesus loved," who was the founder and guiding genius of the Johannine community.

While the fact of the uniqueness of John's Gospel is evident, it is not at all clear how this Gospel came to be unique. Raymond Brown has attempted to reconstruct the origin and development of the historical Christian community out of which the Fourth Gospel came. He concludes that this community began its unique journey when Samaritan converts entered it and brought with them elements of Samaritan thought, including a christology which was not centered on a Davidic Messiah. Because of the long-standing animosity between Jews and Samaritans, the latter came to look for a Messiah who would bring a saving revelation directly from God. They looked, therefore, beyond David to the prophet promised by God to Moses: "I will raise up for them a prophet like you from among their own people; I will put my words in the mouth of the prophet, who shall speak to them everything that I command" (Deut 18:18). Such an expectation would be reflected in the words of the woman of Samaria, when she said to Jesus, "When he [the Messiah] comes, he will proclaim all things to us" (John 4:25). Brown concludes that these Samaritan converts acted as a catalyst as they "brought with them categories for interpreting Jesus that launched the Johannine community toward a theology of descent from above and pre-existence" (*The Community of the Beloved Disciple,* 45).

I am inclined to agree with Brown as far as he goes. However, I am not convinced that the mere discovery of new categories for describing the coming of the Messiah is sufficient to explain the very special character of John's Gospel. My own conclusion is that this community, under the guidance of the

Beloved Disciple, was already so *mystically* inclined that it was predisposed to adopt a christology that would emphasize the divine reality in Jesus as the eternal Word made flesh. One would expect to find such an awareness in a mystical community for whom the divine presence is felt so intensely that the whole world seems to be transparent. This would account for the emphasis in the Fourth Gospel on the divinity of Jesus and the absence there of many episodes that reflect his human nature, such as the agony in the Garden of Gethsemane.

In this regard I have benefited greatly from L. William Countryman's book, *The Mystical Way in the Fourth Gospel.* He would certainly agree with Sandra Schneiders (as noted above) that critical scholarship is at an impasse when it comes to appreciating fully the highly symbolic nature of John's Gospel. In fact, he writes: "One might find reason to suggest that modern analytical scholarship has made us uneasy about studying the specifically religious or mystical wellsprings of early Christianity" (*The Mystical Way in the Fourth Gospel,* 2nd ed., 2). Moreover, Schneiders herself has noted that "the spirituality of John's Gospel is essentially mystical and contemplative, giving rise to a theology that is very little concerned with institution and very much concerned with union and life. For this reason it has always been the favorite Gospel of the church's mystics" (*Written That You May Believe,* 47).

In the presentations that follow, we will have ample opportunity to deal with aspects of Johannine thought that clearly move beyond the realm of merely scientific interpretation, although that will always be the starting point. We will note, in particular, John's special concern for a religious experience that goes beyond religious rituals, titles, and formulas and which is never satisfied with less than a profound mystical experience of God, in Jesus Christ and through the ministry of the Spirit.

We are well aware that "going beyond" a scientifically established interpretation of Scripture may also mean engaging in purely subjective and arbitrary interpretation. We must be concerned, therefore, about the safeguards that may protect us from such an abusive treatment of Scripture. In the first place, a proper spiritual interpretation will always grow out of the literal meaning as established by scientific methodology. The Vatican Instruction clearly indicates how this should happen: "care must be taken to avoid a one-sided approach that would restrict itself, on the one hand, to a spiritual commentary empty of historical-critical grounding or, on the other, to an historical-critical commentary lacking doctrinal or spiritual content" (*The Interpretation of the Bible in the Church,* 31–2). Beyond that, the best guidance will be the experience of the actual community of believers, as assessed by a living magisterium, which is sensitive to both scholarly and pastoral concerns. Such ecclesiastical guidance may seem restrictive at times, but it is at least as valid as any relatively isolated guild of scholars.

Appreciating Biblical Events

Our modern culture is intensely verbal. We process words with amazing speed and we are bombarded by them in all the media. We should not be surprised, therefore, to learn that scientific study of the Bible is also devoted almost exclusively to an analysis of biblical words. At the same time, it is clear that the deepest and richest meaning of the Bible is found only in the biblical *events* toward which those words point.

The Bible is, first and foremost, a history of salvation. It is, therefore, in crucial saving events, representing God's decisive action in our history, that we will find the real meaning of the Scriptures. And it is only there that we will find the biblical wisdom, which tells us about the meaning and purpose of our own existence. Study of the biblical words remains indispensable but we will miss their deeper meaning if we do not see that they are really interpreting great biblical events. Of course, we know that God is constantly acting decisively in our history but there are certain crucial and creative moments when a whole new impetus is given to the flow of time.

There is no doubt that the biblical words have a worthwhile meaning independent of the events of the Bible. The same can be said of the sayings of Confucius or of other great religious philosophers. The point is that the *full and salvific* meaning of the biblical words cannot be grasped unless they are seen in connection with the events to which they refer and whose meaning they reveal. What then is this deeper and more authentic meaning of the Bible to which the words point and which alone constitutes true biblical interpretation? It is the meaning that we discover when we realize that all the biblical words are anchored in and flow from the central biblical events of *Exodus* for the Hebrew Scriptures and of the *death and resurrection of Jesus* for the New Testament.

We constantly need to remind ourselves that not a single word of the Hebrew Scriptures (the Christian Old Testament) was written before the Exodus of the Hebrew slaves from the bondage of the Pharaoh, which occurred about 1250 B.C.E., and that not a single word of the New Testament was written before the resurrection of Jesus, which occurred about 30 C.E. We can only speculate about what the thoughts and words of biblical writers might have been prior to those pivotal events. But we can be sure that any thoughts or words that they might have had were changed in the most radical way by these central events of the Bible. We can be sure that, if Peter had kept a diary during the public ministry of Jesus, it would have been very different from what he understood and wrote after the resurrection! It is no exaggeration to say that the events of the Exodus and of the resurrection of Jesus changed forever the meaning of the flow of history, just as a barrel of dye poured into a river will change its color for miles downstream.

All of this can, of course, be grasped on an intellectual level and one may be willing to concede that this point of view has its own significance. It should be noted, however, that this centrality of biblical events has profound and far-reaching implications for the very manner in which one accepts biblical revelation and guides one's life by it. For if one understands that the deepest meaning of revelation is in the events themselves, the words of Scripture will be seen as subservient to those events since their task will be simply to comment on the events and to draw out of them all the rich implications for one's life. Moreover, it will no longer be sufficient to learn the meaning of the words as such; one will need also to see their meaning in relation to the saving events that they serve.

Personal Integrity Required

At this point, it is important to note the crucial difference between the manner in which one arrives at the meaning of biblical words as distinguished from biblical events. To understand the words, one must be reasonably intelligent and have access to at least some of the aids available for dealing with the language of an ancient book. To understand the meaning of biblical events, however, it is necessary to approach these stories in a condition of *personal honesty and integrity.* For these biblical events are the most real events in human history and only those who are in some measure in touch with the reality of their own lives will ever be able to enter experientially into the meaning of these events.

In other words, one cannot really understand the meaning of the Exodus and the resurrection of Jesus unless one has been able to acknowledge bondage in one's own life and has begun to learn how to move toward freedom. This seems to be the import of the words of the Vatican Instruction mentioned above, for we read there, "Access to a proper understanding of biblical texts is only granted to the person who has an affinity with what the text is saying *on the basis of life experience*" (*The Interpretation of the Bible in the Church,* 21, emphasis added).

It follows that one of the principal obstacles to biblical interpretation is our tendency to live in illusion of one kind or another. To the extent that this is true, we remain mere spectators who hear about the biblical events of liberation from bondage but cannot participate in that experience. This happens because it is so painful to acknowledge need, and therefore illusion becomes most attractive. When Jesus said, "Blessed are you who are poor" (Luke 6:20), he was not extolling poverty as such but declaring instead the good fortune of those who are so powerless that they cannot afford the illusion of seeking freedom through their own efforts alone. This is the reality, and only those who can embrace this reality will be rewarded with the Kingdom.

It should be obvious, then, that one can study the Bible endlessly and still be living in the illusion of one's own control of life, or of the complete sufficiency of one's human knowledge. Indeed, it is a tragic possibility that the most brilliant and powerful ones of this earth are more likely to be deluded by their apparent control of life and will thus be rendered incapable of grasping fully the significance of the great biblical events of liberation. Knowledge is a wonderful possession as long as it is profound enough to know that the most important areas of human life have a mysterious dimension that is quite impervious to the probing of human reason. Therefore, a little knowledge with true humility leads to greater wisdom than superior knowledge crippled by the illusion of prideful self-sufficiency. On the other hand, smug ignorance is certainly no friend of the Bible. What is needed is profound knowledge that knows its limits.

Locating the Mystery

I shall always be grateful for a lesson taught me by my theology professor, Fr. Cipriano Vagaggini, O.S.B. He pointed out that the true role of biblical and theological science is not to reduce, much less to destroy, the divine mystery in human life, but to *locate* it. Such a scholarly enterprise will assess the authentic characteristics of divine mystery in human life and will evaluate the fruits produced by contact with that mystery. Though the mysterious presence of God among us cannot be fully analyzed or controlled by human reason, the fruits in human attitudes and behavior can readily reveal the authenticity of that presence. The great mystic Teresa of Avila is supposed to have said that if she had to choose, she would prefer a theologian to a saint for her confessor. The clear implication is that the theologian would be better equipped to help her discern the nature and consequences of God's presence in her moments of mystical transport.

Vagaggini was well aware that one of the pitfalls of biblical interpretation is a false sense of one's ability to study the Bible in a way that ignores the mysterious presence of God in it or refuses to consult good theology in identifying the dimensions of that presence. Otherwise, one is always in danger of finding a "divine mystery" of one's own making, or one created by a misguided leader, in which case the consequences are inevitably tragic. One need look no farther than the Heaven's Gate cult for evidence of this danger. Their mass suicide may have seemed in a sense heroic but it was tragically out of touch with the reality of a God who is loving and compassionate.

I have found it helpful at times to offer my students a graphic illustration of the biblical project of locating the divine mystery in the text and in our lives. Let us imagine that the thousands of words of the Bible are an outer circle, a kind of verbal galaxy, which we encounter when we first approach the Bible. All biblical scholarship is concerned with the meaning of these words and the importance of wrestling with the words is indisputable. However, there is an inner circle also, which we reach by going beyond the words to the great saving events of the Exodus and the resurrection of Jesus. As we have noted already, the deepest meaning of the Bible is found on this level, and this meaning is available only where there is real faith and personal honesty. For assistance at this stage, one must turn to prayer and, on the human level, to a spiritual director or a trusted friend. Finally, at the very center of these circles, there is the divine mystery itself which, for Christians, is represented by the person of Jesus Christ. When one reaches this heart of the Bible, it is time for worship in loving contemplation.

The Passion Story Is Central

In view of what has been already said, it should not be surprising to learn that the passion, death, and resurrection of

Jesus constitute the heart and soul of all divine revelation. For this is the crucial event toward which all other words and events point. In fact, it has often been noted that the Gospels were written backwards, in the sense that the first stage of gospel formation was nothing more than a summary of the passion story. A classic example of this is found in 1 Corinthians 15:3-5, where Paul provides a capsule of his preaching: "that Christ died for our sins . . . that he was buried, that he was raised . . . and that he appeared. . . ." This narrative is presented by Paul as the quintessence of gospel revelation and one will note immediately that it is a series of events, and not some saying of Jesus, that is at the center. No doubt a saying of Confucius is central to his teaching, but for Christianity all is centered in the event of Jesus' death and resurrection.

Only at a second stage did the evangelists add the stories and sayings of the public ministry of Jesus. Moreover, they were necessarily highly selective in this process as they chose those episodes and sayings of Jesus which were seen to be significant, not just at the time they occurred, but especially in the light of the death and resurrection of Jesus. Accordingly, it is clear that certain actions or sayings of Jesus, which seemed to be important during his ministry, were seen later to have been really insignificant, while other apparently unimpressive events or sayings were later recognized as indispensable because they showed how Jesus made choices which led to his untimely death and his glorious victory. Such choices were seen to be important because it was understood that the followers of Jesus would have to make similar decisions in their own lives.

It is also noteworthy that the death and resurrection of Jesus happened on the anniversary of the original Exodus. This could not have been an accident, for it expressed the conviction of the gospel writers that the death and resurrection of Jesus summed up and transcended the meaning of the Exodus from Egypt. And just as the continuous actuality of the Exodus is expressed in the annual Passover meal of Judaism, so also the Christian Eucharist has been understood as the continuous representation of the reality and consequences of the death and resurrection of Jesus. For this reason, the Easter Vigil Eucharist takes on special significance, for it celebrates the Paschal event on the actual anniversary of its occurrence.

John's Special Concern

As we ponder the Fourth Gospel, we become more and more aware that its author has a special concern, which governs the way in which he presents the story of Jesus and of our salvation. This Gospel was written several decades after the Synoptic Gospels and it is evident that the author has noticed something happening in the Christian communities that is a source of deep concern to him.

It is clear in all the Gospels, as it is in the entire Bible, that salvation is offered to us humans in a *sacramental* way. We are made up of body and spirit and therefore our contacts with God will inevitably be expressed in a way that respects this reality. Jesus himself, as Word made flesh, becomes the primary and essential sacramental contact between humans and their God. This also means that religious expression will always involve ritual words and actions. Indeed, the great saving events of the Exodus and resurrection of Jesus have always been re-enacted in a sacramental way in both Israel's Passover and in the Christian Eucharist. We are not angels and we should not act toward God as if we were pure spirits. Nor does God act toward us in that way.

John's special concern seems to derive from the fact that Christians of his day already had begun to succumb to that most dangerous temptation of sacramental religion, namely, the careful observance of ritual without that deep, spiritual counterpart that constitutes the true meaning and purpose of the ritual. This temptation is so dangerous because it is so much easier to observe rituals than to undertake personal conversion. Meticulous concern with external appearances may provide the illusion of virtue while inner conversion to unselfish love and service may be largely absent. As a consequence, we note throughout the Gospel of John an attempt to warn against a superficial Christianity, that knows all the right theological words and performs all the right ritual actions but which has not discovered the rich personal and mystical union with God in Christ for which these words and actions exist and toward which they point.

And so, for example, when John writes about baptism, he plays down the water ritual in order to emphasize the living faith, which alone makes the ritual effective for salvation. This is true also of his discussion of the Eucharist, where he moves the institution of this primary sacrament out of the Last Supper in order to provide a lengthy introduction where he can stress the need for a deeply personal faith if the sacrament is to be fruitful in the lives of its recipients. Moreover, this authentic faith will always involve to some degree a profound mystical awareness of God's presence in even the most ordinary moments of our lives. This concern for a personal mystical experience of the presence of God, centered in Christ and nurtured by the Spirit, will be seen in every part of John's Gospel.

Jesus and the Community of John

One of the most striking features of John's Gospel is the tendency to identify Jesus with the community itself. No doubt the mystical quality of the author's experience was a major factor here, for mysticism tends to disregard the limits of time and space. Thus, in chapter 4, Jesus is pictured converting the Samaritan woman and her villagers, yet there is no evidence elsewhere that any Samaritans became followers of Jesus during his public ministry. This beautiful story puts us in touch, therefore, with a historical event, which has been narrated in a way that sensitively accommodates the interests of the Samaritan converts in the Johannine community.

Likewise, in chapter 9, the parents of the blind man refuse to testify before the Pharisees about their son lest they be cast out of the synagogue (9:22). In fact, it is extremely unlikely that anyone was expelled from the synagogue during the public ministry of Jesus. On the contrary, Jesus himself, according to Luke 4:16-18, was not only admitted to the synagogue at Nazareth but was invited to read and comment on a biblical text. Once again, the experience of the community of John at the end of the first century, when they were in fact being expelled from the synagogue, is read back into the context of the ministry of Jesus.

Finally, and most importantly, the community of John sees itself standing with Jesus before Pilate during the passion of Jesus. It is very likely that this community was located in Asia Minor where, according to the book of Revelation, they experienced radical weakness in the presence of Roman power, just as Jesus did before Pilate. They too felt the humiliation of Jesus as he was mocked and scourged. And they too knew by faith that the real power lay in the love of Jesus, just as must also be the case in their own situation. The primary purpose of John's Gospel will be to reveal the power of this love, which Jesus brings from the Father and offers to us.

1

The Hour Has Come

It is admittedly unusual to begin reflections on a gospel with a discussion of the story of the passion, death, and resurrection of Jesus. The evangelist certainly expected his readers to start at the beginning of the Gospel and that is, of course, what should normally be done. However, if one wishes to follow a thematic approach, rather than a chapter-by-chapter commentary, it makes sense to follow the process of the Gospel's actual composition. That means beginning with the earliest stage of gospel formation, which is the story of the last crucial days in the life of Jesus.

Such a way of proceeding is almost mandatory when one reflects upon the fact that it was only in the dying and rising of their master that the disciples actually came to a clear understanding of his person and mission. Nor did this dramatic outcome of his life amount to some minor adjustments. It was in fact an almost total reevaluation of everything that they had experienced in the days before his death. They had clearly expected Jesus to be a political messiah who would drive out the hated Roman occupiers of their land and restore the glory of a

Davidic reign featuring national dignity and independence. It gradually became obvious to the disciples that Jesus was not pursuing that path, and then their bewilderment turned to dismay as they saw their beloved master put to death in the most painful and shameful way. But then he appeared to them alive and victorious. At that moment they began to understand how God's way had canceled their own human plans and that, in place of a merely human messiah, they now had a divine and glorious savior. This was the beginning of God's revelation for them and, as we have already noted, all the rest of the New Testament was written in the light of that glorious event. Thus, the passion story will always be the heart of the meaning of Jesus, for the disciples and for ourselves.

"They planned to put him to death" (11:53)

It has been customary to divide John's Gospel in a way that places the beginning of John's passion story at chapter 13. However, there seem to be compelling reasons to locate the beginning of that story already at the end of chapter 11. According to John's Gospel, the raising of Lazarus (11:1-44) precipitated a crisis among the temple authorities, who immediately began to make plans to eliminate Jesus as an intolerable threat to their way of life. We read:

> So the chief priests and the Pharisees called a meeting of the council and said, "What are we to do? This man is performing many signs. If we let him go on like this, everyone will believe in him, and the Romans will come and destroy both our holy place and our nation." But one of them, Caiphas, who was high priest that year, said to them, "You know nothing at all! You do not understand that it is better for you to have one man die for the people than to have the whole nation destroyed" (11:47-50).

We recall that the Synoptic Gospels also begin their passion stories by noting that the temple authorities were conspiring to put Jesus to death. Thus, we read in Mark 14:1, "The chief priests and the scribes were looking for a way to arrest Jesus by stealth and kill him . . ." (see also Matt 26:3-4 and Luke 22:2). Thus, all the passion stories agree that Jesus' last days begin with a decision on the part of the Jewish hierarchy that they should reject the messianic claims of anyone who challenged their power structure and who showed no interest in cooperating with their perception of how the Messiah should govern Israel. There will be a trial later before the high priest, but the decision has already been made.

"The house was filled with the fragrance of the perfume" (12:3)

This recognition that John's passion story begins earlier than chapter 13 seems to be confirmed by the fact that an anointing of Jesus follows immediately, just as it does in Mark 14:3-9 and in Matthew 26:6-13. The story of the anointing in John's Gospel, though quite different from that of Mark and Matthew, is obviously the same basic story. The best explanation is that John found it in the tradition and modified it to suit his own purposes. Thus, the scene is at Bethany, as in Mark and Matthew, but the unidentified woman now becomes Mary, sister of Lazarus, while Martha too is given a part to play. Judas has the villain's role as he takes the place of those who objected to such a "waste" of precious ointment. However, it is Mary's role that is crucial.

In the story of the raising of Lazarus, which we will visit later, Mary represents the Johannine community as she is given the symbolic role of one who, like that community, has a special mystical relationship with Jesus. And Martha in turn represents other early Christian communities who are very dutiful in their devotion to ritual and doctrine but are judged not to have achieved that ideal status. In the story of the anointing, therefore, Mary is again the favored one who anoints the feet of Jesus and dries them with her hair (borrowing an element from a similar gospel story found in Luke 7:38). These discrepancies will disturb us only if we fail to realize that John is far more concerned here with symbolism than with history.

The polar opposite of Mary is not Martha, of course, but Judas. He cannot follow Jesus into the uncontrollable world of unselfish love. His aims are far too venal and political. Therefore, he leads the chorus of criticism at the supposed foolishness of Mary in anointing Jesus' feet with precious ointment. But, just as in Mark's account, Jesus rebukes him and defends the actions of Mary as being most appropriate under the circumstances: "Leave her alone. She bought it so that she might keep it for the day of my burial" (12:7). Mark says that she was actually anointing him for burial (14:8), but the connection with the death of Jesus is the same.

I believe that the explanation of this story, which I proposed in an earlier book, is valid here also (see *Flowers in the Desert,* 150–1). In fact, this episode is so important to the passion story precisely because it represents in miniature what Jesus is about to do in the climactic last days of his life on earth. Mary performs an act of loving kindness, which, from a merely rational perspective, is extravagant and foolish; Jesus will do the same when he anoints all of us with the precious ointment of his lifeblood on Calvary. This alerts us immediately to the fact that the passion story is far more about the loving of Jesus than about his suffering. Indeed, his suffering is the consequence of his loving. Jesus defends the action of Mary and calls it "a beautiful deed" (Mark 14:6, author's translation), just as the Father will make known to all believers that what Jesus did, though apparently foolish, is the most beautiful and significant event in all human history.

Those who imitate Jesus through a life of loving service to others will also be thought foolish, but eventually all will know that wisdom is on their side. Moreover, just as through the anointing of Jesus "the house was filled with the fragrance of the perfume" (12:3), so also our anointing by Jesus fills the universe with a fragrance of divine love beyond imagining. There is little doubt that the community of John believed that their mystical appreciation of Jesus was also a source of special fragrance in their own world.

"Hosanna!" (12:13)

John draws upon the common tradition also for his brief reference to the triumphant entry of Jesus into Jerusalem although he places it later in the sequence of events than the other evangelists (cf. Mark 11:1-10 and parallels). According to John's version, the crowd acclaims Jesus because of the raising of Lazarus. But when they turn against him at the trial before Pilate, it will be obvious that they interpreted the miracle of the raising of Lazarus as an act of worldly power. They acclaim him a king, therefore, only because they are looking for a powerful political messiah. When they discover that his power is in the vulnerability of his loving, they feel betrayed and angrily reject him.

The Pharisees also mistake the nature of the power of Jesus. They see it only as a threat to their own very limited influence. However, since that is the only power they trust, they have little choice but to defend it. They exaggerate the danger in order to justify their opposition to Jesus. "Look, the whole world has gone after him!" (12:19). John is very adept in pointing out the irony in the situation of Jesus, who is bound to disappoint those who trust only worldly power, because the only power that interests him is the power of love which, in the long term, easily eclipses all other forms of power.

"The hour has come for the Son of Man to be glorified" (12:23)

We recall that John's Gospel refers more than once to the "hour" of Jesus, which will be the climax of his mission on earth. Prior to chapter 12, the "hour" is said to have not yet arrived. Thus, in the dialogue between Jesus and his mother at Cana, he responds to her request with the words, "my hour has not yet come" (2:4). And on two other occasions it is noted that Jesus could not be arrested because his hour had not yet come (7:30 and 8:20). When Jesus says, therefore, that his hour has now arrived, it is a clear indication that he is entering upon the climactic last act of his earthly mission and that, as we have noted, the passion story has already begun.

The unusual circumstances of this dramatic statement are well worth noting:

> Now among those who went up [to Jerusalem] to worship at the festival were some Greeks. They came to Philip, who was from Bethsaida in Galilee, and said to him, "Sir, we wish to see Jesus." Philip went and told Andrew; then Andrew and Philip went and told Jesus. Jesus answered them, "The hour has come for the Son of Man to be glorified" (12:20-23).

Several elements in this passage deserve a comment: first, the "Greeks" mentioned are probably not ethnic Greeks, who would scarcely have been interested in worshiping at the temple, but rather Greek-speaking Jews from some territory outside of Israel. Second, they would have approached Philip because he came from a cosmopolitan city and had a Greek name, which undoubtedly meant that they felt more comfortable with him. All of this is significant for John because he wants us to see that the arrival of that decisive "hour" is in response to the readiness of the larger world for the message of Jesus. This larger world would include, of course, the community of John where the language and milieu were representative of a Christianity that had broken out of its Jewish matrix. (For further discussion of this, see L. Wm. Countryman, *The Mystical Way in the Fourth Gospel*, 2nd ed., 91.)

After Jesus announces the arrival of the fateful "hour" of his final trial and triumph, he immediately offers one of the most significant and profound analogies in any gospel concerning the meaning of his life on this earth: "Very truly, I tell you, unless a grain of wheat falls into the earth and dies, it remains just a single grain; but if it dies, it bears much fruit" (12:24). The single grain of wheat, symbolizing any individual human being, is presumed to have an instinct for survival that would prompt it to struggle mightily to remain intact. But the moisture and warmth cause it to swell and to produce a sprout, so that eventually the original grain becomes nothing more than an empty husk. In a similar way, the follower of Jesus must choose to imitate him by ignoring the instinct of self-preservation in order to be available in loving service to others. It may appear that this will leave only an empty husk of self-hood but Jesus assures us that such a choice will lead to a fruit-fulness and joy that could never be achieved by even the most determined human efforts.

"Now my soul is troubled" (12:27)

Jesus himself proceeds then to become the seed that gives its own life for the sake of the life and happiness of many others. He says that his heart is troubled and that he is tempted to ask the Father to change the script, but he responds quickly, "No, it is for this reason that I have come to this hour. Father, glorify your name" (12:27-28). The Father's name will be glorified when, through the loving obedience of Jesus, it becomes evident to all that the Father is not just powerful but also gentle and compassionate beyond compare. In a biblical context, glorification means to reveal the hidden nature of someone. Thus, Jesus asks for his own glorification (12:23), which will happen, not primarily through resurrection, as we might expect, but through his ultimate self-giving in crucifixion. That will serve as proof positive that his sole motivation was love of others.

It is easy to see that these words of Jesus parallel the Gethsemane scene in the Synoptic Gospels (see Mark 14:32-42). Of course, in John's Gospel the divinity of Jesus is so prominent that all references to human agony are removed and the acceptance by Jesus of the Father's will is expressed with the simple statement, "Father, glorify your name" (12:28). It is the supreme love of Jesus, expressed in his total self-giving, that will reveal the supreme love of the Father also. For it is evident everywhere in John's Gospel that the glorification of the Father is the revelation of his innermost nature.

The response from heaven: "I have glorified it, and I will glorify it again" (12:28) is reminiscent of the voice from heaven reported by the Synoptic Gospels at the baptism and transfiguration of Jesus (Mark 1:11 and 9:7). However, in

John's account, Jesus does not need to be reassured and thus the words from heaven are said to be solely for the edification of the bystanders (12:30).

"And I, when I am lifted up from the earth, will draw all people to myself" (12:32)

The loving self-sacrifice of Jesus, through his being lifted up in crucifixion, will draw all people to him because nothing is more attractive or compelling than an expression of love, and no love is expressed more perfectly than that of Jesus. Unfortunately, many of us still find it difficult to understand the meaning of Jesus' sacrifice because we find it so hard to embrace the unselfishness that the love of Jesus implies. The clear and tragic implication is that there is nothing more that Jesus can do to prove his love for us. And so he sees himself in the same sad situation of Isaiah whose prophetic message was also ignored: "He has blinded their eyes and hardened their heart, so that they might not look with their eyes, and understand with their heart and turn—and I would heal them" (Isa 6:9-10; John 12:40). God permits this blindness because his goodness will not interfere with our human freedom. And so our sinfulness will often amount to squandering the best opportunity in our lives.

"You also ought to wash one another's feet" (13:14)

John signals the intensification of the process of Jesus' final drama with the words: "Now before the festival of the Passover, Jesus knew that his hour had come to depart from this world and go to the Father. Having loved his own who were in the world, he loved them to the end" (13:1). A significant moment in this drama is a final meal with his disciples. It must have been an emotional as well as an intimate experience. John gives us no details about the meal itself, but he does tell us that Jesus surprises the disciples by performing a service of love for them. After he has washed their feet, he explains his unusual action, leaving nothing to chance:

Do you know what I have done to you? You call me Teacher and Lord—and you are right, for that is what I am. So if I, your Lord and Teacher, have washed your feet, you also ought to wash one another's feet. For I have set you an example, that you also should do as I have done to you (13:12-15).

This act of humble service anticipates the passion of Jesus when he will, figuratively speaking, wash the feet of all human beings. And he tells his disciples (and us) that such loving service will do more for the welfare of the human race than all the power that we humans seek and cherish.

After the foot washing Jesus identifies his betrayer and Judas leaves the loving circle of light to enter the cold darkness outside (13:30). Those who have read the passion story in the Synoptic Gospels will notice immediately that the institution of the Eucharist is missing from John's account of the Last Supper. This could not have been an oversight and, in fact, we will see that John has moved the institution of the Eucharist to chapter 6, for reasons that will be discussed at that point. In place of the Eucharist account, he has inserted this story of the foot washing which has the same meaning as the Eucharist, since both are examples of loving service. The Eucharist expresses the self-giving of Jesus through the breaking of the bread (his Body) and the pouring out of the wine (his Blood). This profound action is joined, in the Holy Thursday liturgy, with the powerful symbolic action of the foot washing in a wonderful summary of the meaning of Jesus' life among us. This represents the "secret" which Jesus reveals to us and which, if lived courageously through Good Friday, will lead to the glorious victory of Easter Sunday.

After the foot washing, we find in John's Gospel a lengthy "farewell discourse," which begins at 13:31 and continues to the end of chapter 17. It seems preferable for our purposes to consider these final words of Jesus only after the theme of the Gospel has been revealed in the passion story itself. This makes good sense, I think, since this discourse is concerned essentially with the important and difficult question of how the loving example of Jesus can be translated in the lives and actions of his followers—something that presupposes the dying and rising of Jesus and the sending of the Spirit.

2

Testifying to the Truth

As we have seen, John summarizes the early stages of the traditional passion story. However, he greatly expands the account of the trial of Jesus before Pilate, devoting no less than twenty-nine verses to this subject. It is there that we will find the *central theme* that governs John's perspective throughout his Gospel. But first we must see how he leads up to that decisive moment in the passion story.

"So the soldiers . . . arrested Jesus and bound him" (18:12)

John tells us that Jesus went with his disciples across the Kidron Valley (just east of Jerusalem) to a garden, which is obviously the Garden of Gethsemane. John makes no reference to an agony at this point but notes simply that soldiers came with Judas to arrest Jesus. The service that Judas offered the authorities was information about where Jesus could be found and, once located, how he could be identified. In John's version, there is no need for Judas to embrace and kiss the master in order to identify him because Jesus himself comes forward and tells them who he is. For John, Jesus is in charge and willingly offers himself for judgment and death. This is meant to emphasize his free and deliberate self-giving as proof of his love.

When Peter makes a halfhearted effort to protect him, Jesus tells him, "Put your sword back into its sheath. Am I not to drink the cup that the Father has given me?" (18:11). This reminds us that Jesus is not going to his death as a helpless victim but rather that he sees his dying as the final act in a life of unselfish love and as an act that will reveal also the love of his heavenly Father. Upon reflection, we realize that for us too every unselfish act is a little dying and that the final moment of death becomes simply the last and best opportunity to let go of one's own plans and wishes for the sake of God's call. In this regard, we are simply asked to follow the lead of Jesus himself. For when he submits to being arrested and bound, he is exercising the freedom to love which is most often expressed in an experience of bondage to the needs of others. "So the soldiers, their officer, and the Jewish police arrested Jesus and bound him" (18:12).

"They took him to Annas, who was the father-in-law of Caiphas, the high priest that year" (18:13)

In view of the varying accounts of Jesus' appearance before the high priests and the Jewish council, the most likely sequence of events is that there was, first, a kind of informal hearing before the retired high priest, Annas, for fact-finding purposes. This brief encounter would have been followed, later that evening or early the next morning, by a formal trial before the incumbent high priest, Caiphas, and the council of elders. In John's very sketchy version, the trial before Caiphas is not even mentioned, and the appearance before Annas shows a Jesus who is far from compliant. In effect, he asks Annas where he has been that he does not know already about his work and teaching. It is clear that this religious trial is of little importance to John since it appears to have been nothing more than the confirmation of a decision that has already been made. He wishes to move quickly to the trial before Pilate, which is the stage on which Jesus will define most clearly the whole purpose of his earthly mission.

Before we come to that stage, however, we must take note of John's relatively brief reference to Peter's denial of Jesus. John recalls, with the Synoptics, that there were three denials and that it all ended with a cockcrow. The consistent emphasis on the cockcrow in all the Gospels elevates it, I think, to a symbolic level of meaning. In the days before alarm clocks, most people rose at dawn when the cocks began to crow. This cockcrow should be recognized, therefore, as an "awakening" of Peter to the reality of his human weakness. This painful acceptance of reality in his life allowed him then to seek and find forgiveness, which will be noted in John's Gospel in chapter 21, where Peter "cancels" his denials by declaring three times his love for Jesus.

"Then they took Jesus from Caiphas to Pilate's headquarters" (18:28)

As we have noted, John devotes no less than twenty-nine verses to the trial of Jesus before Pilate and this fact alone alerts us to the importance of this stage in his passion story. It is, quite simply, from a *theological* perspective, the very center of the Fourth Gospel. Obviously, the dying and rising of Jesus constitute the *historical* center but the *theological meaning* of those events will be revealed in the interaction between Jesus and Pilate.

Scholars have long noted the careful literary structure of this section of John's Gospel and they have generally recognized here an example of the literary device called a "chiasmus." This term derives from the Greek letter, "chi," which is written like a large "X" and thus suggests a crossing pattern. Accordingly, the Oxford English Dictionary defines a chiasmus as: "A grammatical figure by which the order of the words in one of two parallel clauses is inverted in the other." When applied to the seven scenes of the trial before Pilate, this means that scenes one and seven will be related, as will also scenes two and six, as well as three and five. This also draws special attention to scene four, which is in a sense the hinge between the other scenes. Such a literary structure is used to provide a sense of symmetry, much appreciated in the ancient world, and to create an internal dynamism, which serves to highlight elements which are central to the narrative.

In the case of the trial of Jesus before Pilate, it seems evident that John modified the historical sequence of episodes in order to achieve this effect. Thus, for example, the scourging and mocking of Jesus, which belongs more properly, as in the Synoptics, immediately before the way of the cross, is moved to an earlier stage so that it becomes the pivotal "hinge" scene in the chiastic arrangement. Johannine structuring is revealed also in the fact that scenes one and seven are *outside* Pilate's headquarters, as are also scenes three and five, whereas scenes two and six are *inside* the headquarters. All this is of interest only because it has some bearing on the meaning of each scene, as we shall see.

Scene One (18:28-32): *"We are not permitted to put anyone to death"* (18:31)

This scene is concerned with the charges brought against Jesus at Pilate's headquarters. Pilate, as Roman procurator, normally resided at Caesarea on the seacoast. He had come to Jerusalem for this major feast, not for religious reasons, but to take personal charge of a situation that was always volatile and could easily lead to rioting—something about which Rome would have been very sensitive.

The Jewish authorities remain outside the headquarters to avoid ritual defilement through contact with the secular and profane presence of this hated foreign power in their land. At some point these authorities are joined by a crowd, who are there, not because of Jesus, but to remind Pilate of the custom of releasing a prisoner as part of the celebration of a major feast. Jesus is handed over to Pilate but he must come to the outer courtyard to discover the reason for their bringing a prisoner to him: "What accusation do you bring against this man" (18:29)?

The Jewish authorities do not respond directly to Pilate's question but declare simply that it should be obvious that they would not bring someone to a Roman court unless he had committed a Roman crime. Pilate cannot resist the temptation to remind them of their limited powers as a subjugated people: "Take him yourselves and judge him according to your law" (18:31). But they want his death and that requires Roman involvement, something that they find most distasteful. This reveals the depth of their fear concerning the threat to their interests posed by Jesus.

We should note here the correspondence of this scene to scene seven where, as we shall see, Pilate comes outside again to address the Jewish authorities but at this point he is finally ready to grant their request for the death of Jesus. From a self-confident and imperious Roman official he has become a fearful and irresponsible judge.

Scene Two (18:33-38a): *"For this I was born, and for this I came into the world, to testify to the truth"* (18:37)

Pilate returns now to the interior of his headquarters, where Jesus is held captive, and asks him if he is in fact the "King of the Jews" (18:33). At this point, no one has claimed such a title for Jesus, but Pilate has apparently deduced that this is in fact the charge against him. After all, the enemies of Jesus know that this is the only charge that would be of any interest to Pilate.

Jesus does not entirely reject the notion that he might be a king and, in fact, both John and his readers know that he is king of heaven and earth. But he is not a king in any earthly political sense: "My kingdom is not from this world" (18:36). There is no doubt, however, that the deeper issue here concerns kingship in the more general sense of *power*. Pilate, as representative of the mighty Roman Empire, wields a power that seems invincible. The presence of his soldiers and the opulence of his palace proclaim this kind of power.

But Jesus, a bound and helpless prisoner, possesses a power that easily eclipses the power of Rome and in fact of all human authority. His power is the apparently unpromising but truly invincible *power of unselfish love*. And so this crucial scene addresses the central issue in John's Gospel: Did Jesus come to bring a divine power that is just another example of the power we assign to wealth and influence, or did he bring a radically new kind of power—the power of love—which is usually expressed in suffering and self-effacement but which easily surpasses every other kind of power? The answer is found in the reply of Jesus to Pilate's question, "So you are a king?" (18:37).

Jesus seems to respond directly to Pilate as he says, "You say that I am a king" (18:37). Of course, Pilate has not said this at all. But John wants Jesus to claim some kind of kingship and some form of power, even if it is far from the kind of kingship and power that Pilate has in mind. Then Jesus states positively the sense in which he is a king and does possess power: *"For this I was born, and for this I came into the world, to testify to the truth"* (18:37, emphasis added). This has to be one of the most significant declarations in John's Gospel. For it states in the clearest terms that the whole purpose of the incarnation, which for John means the divine Word taking on a human nature, is that Jesus may be the one in whom the ultimate and only indispensable *truth* is revealed to us human beings. This is not, of course, philosophical or scientific truth, for Jesus is neither a philosopher nor a scientist; rather, it is a truth that is represented by all the words and deeds of Jesus, indeed by his very being.

The significance of the word, "truth," in John's Gospel is clearly seen in the fact that this noun occurs twenty-five times in his Gospel, and only seven times in the Synoptics. The adjective, "truthful," occurs fourteen times in John and only twice in the Synoptics. In all of these instances, the reference is to the revelation that Jesus brings to us from the heart of his heavenly Father.

This revelation tells us that all real power is centered in the *unselfish loving* that Jesus offered throughout his life and which he will now express perfectly in his self-giving in sacrificial death. This is what the evangelist meant when he said,

"Having loved his own who were in the world, he loved them to the end" (13:1). This second scene in the trial before Pilate presents, therefore, a dramatic contrast between the obvious power of Pilate and the less apparent but much more real power of Jesus. Because of the complete superiority of the power of love in Jesus, he is a true king, though not in the commonly understood sense of often tyrannical human monarchs.

Since the loving power of Jesus is inevitably directed to the benefit of others, it is not surprising that Jesus should continue with the words, *"Everyone who belongs to the truth listens to my voice"* (18:37, emphasis added). To listen to the voice of Jesus means to accept and to trust his words and to guide one's life in accordance with his teaching. We recall that Jesus uses similar language when he compares himself to a good shepherd: "He calls his own sheep by name and leads them out. . . . He goes ahead of them, and the sheep follow him because they know his voice" (10:3-4). These are "his own sheep" whom the Father has entrusted to his care, not in some narrow sense of predestination, but in the sense that the creator has placed within all of us a chord that responds to the call of Jesus, except when that response is blocked by fear or ignorance or selfish concerns.

When by the grace of God we take the risk of trusting the message of Jesus and commit ourselves to his wisdom, we "belong to the truth," that is, we place ourselves under the guidance of his words. This means that, though we recognize the reality of Pilate's kind of power, we acknowledge as supreme the power that Jesus possesses. In fact, political power and the power of wealth are not at all evil in themselves but they become evil and oppressive when they are not placed in the service of the ultimate power of love.

The mystical sensitivity of the Johannine community enables them to recognize with special acuteness the primacy of love in the life and death of Jesus. This awareness is heightened by their own suffering at the hands of those who resolutely refuse to recognize the divinity of Jesus and the consequent total claim that he has on all human beings.

All of this makes no sense at all to Pilate (or to future power brokers). His only reaction is the ambiguous query, "What is truth?" (18:38). John's rather sympathetic presentation of Pilate suggests that this question should not be taken as disdainful or cynical. Rather, Pilate simply asks the only really inescapable question and, like so many, he is too busy or too distracted or too pragmatic to wait for an answer.

The corresponding scene six, in the chiastic scheme, is also concerned with power. By that time, however, Pilate will have clearly and fatally chosen to stay in the world he understands, and thereby loses everything that is worthwhile.

Scene Three (18:38b-40): "I find no case against him" (18:38)

Pilate is a shrewd and experienced politician, and it takes him less than a minute to conclude that Jesus is no threat to him. The very fact that the Jewish authorities charge him with a crime is proof enough that he is not a revolutionary, since there is nothing that those authorities would like more than to be rid of the Romans. Nonetheless, Pilate knows that the Jewish leaders can easily foment a riot and that is something that would not look good on his record in Rome. We can well imagine that Pilate desperately wants a promotion from this troublesome assignment and is ready to calm the waters, no matter the cost.

Pilate's last ploy is an offer to release Jesus in keeping with the custom of freeing a prisoner as a gesture of good will on a festive occasion. Under normal circumstances, they would have gladly accepted this offer. But they will now settle for nothing less than the death of Jesus, and they resolutely refuse to be distracted from that objective. On a deeper level, they too are making a fateful choice in the presence of the truth brought by Jesus. They think that God's truth must be passed on through their narrow religious channels. They cannot risk the flood that Jesus has come to unleash.

And so the authorities reject Pilate's offer to free Jesus and clamor instead for the release of a well-known criminal:

"Not this man, but Barabbas" (18:40). At this point, Pilate realizes that he is no longer really in charge of the situation. The Jewish authorities have put him on the defensive. In fact, however, it is Jesus who is in charge, for he is the only one there who knows exactly what is at stake. He stands in the calm eye of the hurricane, as the powerful winds of ambition, fear, and anger swirl around him.

This scene corresponds to the fifth scene where Pilate will again declare the innocence of Jesus but by then it is no more than a futile gesture since the fate of Jesus is already sealed.

Scene Four (19:1-3): *"They kept coming up to him, saying, 'Hail, King of the Jews'"* (19:3)

In this crucial "hinge" scene, Pilate orders Jesus to be flogged and to be subjected to the taunts and ridicule of the soldiers. Though consisting of only three verses, the import of this scene is most significant. We have already noted that John disregards historical considerations as he moves the flogging and taunting of Jesus from its more likely location just before the way of the cross. This clearly indicates the special importance of this episode for John's understanding of the passion of Jesus.

It is also noteworthy that this is the only scene where Pilate is not personally present. Since he has refused to act as a just judge, his chance to shape history has been lost. His attitude changes after this scene as he is put more and more on the defensive and is even fearful. But most of all, this scene is a dramatic and shocking example of the weakness and vulnerability of Jesus. For he is not only subjected to extreme physical pain but he also suffers the psychic torture of mockery and ridicule.

The taunting of Jesus takes the form of a mockery of his supposed royal pretensions: "And the soldiers wove a crown of thorns and put it on his head, and they dressed him in a purple robe. They kept coming up to him, saying, 'Hail, King of the Jews!'" (19:2-3). All the while, the love of Jesus was never more evident and his true kingship was never more clearly displayed. The divine power of love rarely looks like human power, just as the fragility of human power is often not recognized until it is too late.

No other scene in the Gospel of John portrays so clearly the vulnerability, and the hidden power, of unselfish love. Suddenly, it becomes clear that the most influential people in the world are not the movers and shakers of government and industry but the humble, often obscure, people who have learned how to make the love of Jesus present in their world. As in the case of Jesus, this power will be revealed only at the end, and then its revelation will be incredibly dramatic.

Scene Five (19:4-8): "Pilate said to them, 'Here is the man'" (19:5)

This scene corresponds to scene three and, here again, Pilate goes outside to tell the Jews that he finds Jesus innocent of the charges brought against him: "Look, I am bringing him out to you to let you know that I find no case against him" (19:4). The major difference is that this time he brings Jesus out with him. It has often been assumed that Pilate had Jesus scourged and then presented publicly in a futile attempt to placate his accusers. It would be as if he were saying, Is this not enough punishment?

Such an interpretation may perhaps be historically plausible, but John is far more interested in its theological and symbolic meaning. For Jesus, beaten and bruised, is being presented to us as well as to the crowd outside Pilate's headquarters. And his pitiful condition is intended to remind us of the cost of truly unselfish love.

When Pilate says, "Here is the man" (19:5), he is making a statement whose implications are boundless. It is as if he had said, This is what real love can cost and, although an unbelieving world may be repelled by this, it will soon be evident that the final outcome is stunning victory and glory. It is very likely that the community of John sees itself in this representation of Jesus. It seems quite likely that this community was suffering severely both from Roman persecution and from rejection by their Jewish compatriots. Such a situation would suggest that the community was located in Asia Minor toward the end of the first century. Thus they can readily identify with this "man" whom Pilate presents to the world as misguided and deserving only death. But their faith tells them that they will also be victorious with Jesus as the Roman monuments crumble to dust.

The Jewish authorities also have become for John part of the unbelieving world and therefore cannot recognize the divine (and truly royal) power in this pathetic figure. And so they must destroy what they cannot understand: "Crucify him! Crucify him!" (19:6). Once again, we must remind ourselves that they do not do this because they are Jews but only because they have not been able to accept the message of Jesus. Their successors in this regard will belong to every race and every nation.

Pilate's suggestion that they take him and crucify him themselves is historically unlikely. However, it serves John's purposes as it provides the Jews with an opportunity to express their real grievance against Jesus: "We have a law, and according to the law he ought to die because he has claimed to be the Son of God" (19:7). This is, at last, the religious and true complaint that the Jews have regarding Jesus. Being obviously a human being, he has nonetheless claimed to be divine, which would constitute blasphemy according to the Jewish Law. It is very doubtful that such a clear claim to divinity was made by Jesus during his ministry, but it is being made very clearly by the Johannine community, and it is they who are being rejected and persecuted because of this by their Jewish compatriots.

From the perspective of this Johannine community, Jesus has clearly established his divinity and this should supercede all merely legal objections. In the story of the blind man in John 9, the issue is clearly stated. The Jews appeal to Moses (representing the Law): "We know that God has spoken to Moses, but as for this man, we do not know where he comes from" (9:29). The former blind man, now "seeing" the true nature of Jesus, replies simply, "Here is an astonishing thing! You do not know where he comes form, and yet he opened my eyes" (9:30). There is admittedly a certain logic on the side of the Jews, who clamor for the penalty prescribed for blasphemy. The problem is that this logic has been set on its head by the miraculous power and the new wisdom of Jesus . . . and this spells tragedy for those of all ages who, in spite of the credentials of Jesus, still refuse to believe that everything has changed since his coming.

The reaction of Pilate is surprising: "Now when Pilate heard this, he was more afraid than ever" (19:8). It is unlikely that the historical Pilate would have been frightened, but for John he represents the powerful secular person who cannot be sure that unselfish love is not the only power that really matters. For even the most callous human being is vulnerable at times to the truth that Jesus represents.

As for the Jewish authorities, they represent the equally disastrous situation of powerful religious figures who dare not abandon the neat structures of a religion in which they have invested so much human planning and energy. We hear at this point an echo of the prophetic judgment of Jesus on the religious practices of the Jerusalem temple when he cleansed it of the money changers and animals (2:13-22). Once again, the Jewish authorities are closed to the message of Jesus, not because they are Jews, but because they are human beings who have chosen to use human religious structures to shield themselves from the challenge of Jesus. Unfortunately, they will have successors in every place and time.

Scene Six (19:9-11): *"You would have no power over me unless it had been given you from above"* (19:11)

This scene finds Pilate inside his headquarters once again and it corresponds to the second scene where kingship and power were the subjects of discussion. We must assume that Jesus was brought back into the headquarters where, still dressed as a mock king and covered with wounds, he is asked by Pilate, "Where are you from?" (19:9). As in scene two, the subject is power. Therefore, when Jesus remains silent, Pilate says to him, "Do you refuse to speak to me? Do you not know that I have power to release you, and power to crucify you?" (19:10).

Those who rely on secular or violent power believe to the end that such power solves all problems. They dare not entertain the possibility that some other power may exist. Raymond Brown notes this important distinction: "Pilate has spoken of his physical power over Jesus—he can take Jesus' life away. Jesus speaks to him on another level, the level of truth and of 'genuine' power" (*The Gospel according to John*, vol. 2, 892). As noted above, this truth is the revelation of the supreme power of unselfish love, found in the Father and now made known by Jesus.

There is something almost surreal about the image of Jesus, battered and beaten, replying calmly to the far-from-idle threat of Pilate: "You would have no power over me unless it had been given you from above" (19:11). All power is from God, and the use of power will be judged by God. The supreme power, and the greatest gift of God, is the power of unselfish love. All other power, secular or religious, is meant to be in service of unselfish love. In this scenario, Pilate and the religious authorities represent a power that has been torn loose from love and is therefore doomed. Only the power of Jesus' love, though now appearing vanquished and ridiculous, will prove to be ultimately victorious and liberating.

Scene Seven (19:12-16): *"Then he handed him over to them to be crucified"* (19:16)

This scene corresponds to the first scene where Pilate also comes out to speak to the Jewish authorities. This time, however, it is to grant the request they made in scene one, i.e., to have Jesus put to death. According to the logic of John's account, Pilate grants their request, not because he thinks Jesus is guilty, but because they threaten to denounce him to the emperor: "If you release this man, you are no friend of the emperor" (19:12). This kind of pressure does not excuse Pilate, of course, for he is in fact abdicating his most solemn responsibility, which is to see justice done regardless of pressures or preferences.

(People who lack religious values often find it acceptable to weigh a human life on the scales of convenience and find it dispensable. Stalin is supposed to have chided Roosevelt and Churchill at Yalta when they asked about the reported massacre of ten thousand Polish officers, saying, But there were only ten thousand of them! It is surely true that, when one fails to show respect for a single human being, then all are at risk.)

Having made his fateful decision, Pilate proceeds to render judgment. But first he must proclaim to the Jews (and to the whole world): "Here is your King" (19:14). John wants Pilate to say this because it is true, even though hardly anyone there is aware of it. When they cry out, "Away with him! Away with him! Crucify him!" (19:15), Pilate again says more than he knows, "Shall I crucify your King?" (19:15). When the chief priests answer, "We have no king but the emperor" (19:15), they are rejecting Israel's most fundamental belief in the supremacy of God in human history. Such a stark statement may have been influenced by the Johannine community's later experience of persecution in which they were being denounced to the Roman authorities by members of the synagogue (cf. R. Brown, *The Community of the Beloved Disciple*, 43).

The scene ends with the terribly simple statement: "Then he handed him over to them to be crucified" (19:16). The love of Jesus will now be displayed definitively in his total giving of himself for the sake of others. Without the vision of faith, this would be pure folly and utter defeat. With the vision of faith, it is pure wisdom and total victory. Moreover, this is not just a fact to be noted; it is also an example to be followed.

3

Love Gives All

The story of the crucifixion and death of Jesus is summed up perfectly in the words of John: "Having loved his own who were in the world, he loved them to the end" (13:1). Jesus told Pilate (and all of us) that his coming into the world would reveal the truth about the power of unselfish love. Such love belongs to the very being of God the Father, in whose nature it subsists as the communion of love between Father, Son, and Spirit. This divine love is now made known to us in the Father's sending of the Son into our world. The climax of this revelation is the loving self-sacrifice of Jesus, Son of God, for our salvation. This love is the same power that brought about creation, but it reaches its climax only in the final moments of the life of Jesus. In the apparent weakness and vulnerability of his dying, we discover the most truly powerful act in all human history.

John gives very little attention to the crucifixion itself. Most of his words are devoted to describing, often in symbolic language, the spiritual implications of the dying of Jesus. Once again, one detects a careful chiastic structure in seven scenes. As in the case of the trial before Pilate, this arrangement provides significant comparisons and draws special attention to the fourth or "swing" scene where, as we shall see, Jesus speaks to his mother and the Beloved Disciple.

Scene One (19:16b-18): *"There they crucified him"* (19:18)

In this scene we learn that Jesus was "taken," presumably by the Roman soldiers, and that he was forced to carry his own cross. No mention is made of any help, as in the other gospels, because the Jesus of John's Gospel is clearly in charge and freely gives up his life. The place of the crucifixion is identified as Golgotha and there is mention of two others crucified with him but no special significance is attached to this fact.

When one notes the correspondence of this scene with scene seven, it is clear that the emphasis here is on the lifting up of Jesus in crucifixion, just as in scene seven he is, by contrast, taken down from the cross. This lifting up fulfills the promise of 3:14-15: "And just as Moses lifted up the serpent in the wilderness, so must the Son of Man be lifted up, that whoever believes in him may have eternal life." In that context of baptismal faith, it is clear that the lifting up of Jesus is a sign that challenges all his followers to imitate the love that is most clearly manifested in his total self-giving for the sake of others.

Scene Two (19:19-22): *"It read, 'Jesus of Nazareth, the King of the Jews'"* (19:19)

It was customary in those days to attach a notice to the cross above a crucified person to indicate to passersby the nature of the crime for which he was being punished. This was intended to be a deterrent to others who might be tempted to commit a similar crime. In the case of Jesus, Pilate himself intervenes and orders that a most unusual notice be placed on the cross, by which this Jesus of Nazareth is proclaimed "King of the Jews." He intended it no doubt to be an insult to the Jewish authorities who had insisted on the death of a man he thought was innocent.

Hardly anyone there really believed that Jesus, suffering the fate of a criminal, was in fact the king of Israel. But John wants us to see that Pilate was unwittingly proclaiming the truth about Jesus' identity. Raymond Brown sees here an enthronement of Jesus, which "comes now on the cross when the kingship of Jesus is acknowledged by heraldic proclamation ordered by a representative of the greatest political power on earth and phrased in the sacred and secular language of the time" (*The Gospel according to John*, vol. 2, 919). John is thus very sensitive to the irony in the situation of Jesus who is truly a king because he is exercising the supreme power of love. Yet he never looked less like a king as we humans picture kings. The vision of faith makes all the difference.

Scene Three (19:23-25a): *"Now the tunic was seamless, woven in one piece from the top"* (19:23)

This scene refers specifically to Psalm 22:18: "they divided my clothes among themselves, and for my clothing they cast lots." We recall that it is the first verse of this same psalm that is spoken by Jesus in the other gospel versions of the crucifixion: "My God, my God, why have you forsaken me?" (Mark 15:34). This entire psalm is about the suffering of a just man who is ultimately rescued by God. Some have suggested that John created this scene to fulfill the words of the psalm but that is unlikely since there is no mention in the psalm of a seamless garment, a fact that seems to be the primary focus of the scene.

Many opinions have been voiced concerning the symbolic meaning of the seamless garment. In the first place, it may be a reference to the seamless woven garment worn by the high priest: "They also made the tunics, woven of fine linen, for Aaron and his sons" (Exod 39:27). In that case, it would suggest the priestly role of Jesus. Bearing in mind that the primary function of a priest is to act as mediator between God and humans, Jesus would be performing the supreme act of mediation when he dies on the cross to make God's mercy available to all.

Another possible meaning, fully compatible with the first, is that of unity. The soldiers take pains to preserve the unity of this garment since its value would be greatly reduced if it were cut into pieces. On the symbolic level this would represent the importance of unity among the followers of him who prayed, "that they may all be one" (17:21).

The correspondence of this scene with scene five lies in the fact that we see in that scene the ultimate priestly act of

Jesus who gives up his Spirit to establish a permanent bond between heaven and earth. It is also only through the influence of the Spirit that divisions among humans can be healed and harmony maintained. We will see in chapters 5 and 6 how the Spirit perpetuates the mediating and unifying role of Jesus in the Church.

Scene Four (19:25b-27): *"Woman, here is your Son. . . . Here is your Mother"* (19:26-27)

In the chiastic arrangement of the crucifixion story in John, this scene is the central and pivotal one. This shows how little John is interested in the historical dimension of the crucifixion and how much he wants us to see the powerful spiritual implications of this climactic moment in the life of Jesus. John is in harmony with the other evangelists when he notes the presence of faithful women near the cross, though Mark, wishing to emphasize the isolation of Jesus, says that they "were looking on from a distance" (15:40). No other evangelist, however, makes any reference to the words of Jesus spoken to his mother and to the "disciple whom he loved" (19:26). This unnamed disciple was the founder of the Johannine community and the creator of the unique perspective of that community on the mission of Jesus. Either he, or one of his disciples, was the author of the Fourth Gospel.

There is no doubt that both Mary and the Beloved Disciple were historical characters but it is equally clear that they are presented here in a symbolic sense that transcends their historical significance. We are alerted to this by the unusual way in which Jesus addresses his mother as "woman." And this in turn takes us immediately to the only other place in the Fourth Gospel where the mother of Jesus is mentioned and where he also addresses her as "woman," that is, at the wedding in Cana (2:4).

John seems to see this intimate scene at the cross as a sign of how Jesus prepares for the future when he will no longer be physically present to his disciples. His mother will then represent the Church as the community that will give spiritual birth to subsequent generations of his followers. As such, she will assume the role of second Eve and, just as the first Eve was called "the mother of all living" (Gen 3:20), so Mary will become spiritual mother of all those who believe in her Son. In this sense, she is also aptly called Mother of the Church.

In a similar manner, the Beloved Disciple, representing all faithful Christians, is told to accept Mary as his own mother, just as the faithful followers of Jesus must henceforth look to Mother Church for spiritual nourishment. For it is the Church that makes available that sharing in divine life, which is given through baptism and nourished by the Eucharist.

From this perspective we can also understand why Jesus resisted the initiative of his mother at Cana, when he said, "what concern is that to you and to me?" (2:4). We are told that he did so because his "hour has not yet come" (2:4). In other words, Mary's essential role in salvation must await the final days of Jesus, when his hour will have arrived. At that time, she will participate in his suffering which will become in a sense her birth pangs as she assumes her ultimate role of spiritual mother of Christians, just as she was the physical mother of Jesus.

This dramatic scene is also intended to show how Jesus, at a time of personal agony, is nonetheless thinking of others and is solely concerned with providing for their welfare. In other words, at this moment of extreme weakness, he is exercising the unparalleled power of his unselfish love. This fact directly challenges our secular culture's despair in the presence of weakness and death, just as it reminds us that the possibility of loving continues even when strength begins to ebb and may even be more fruitful than ever before.

Scene Five (19:28-30): *"Then he bowed his head and gave up his spirit"* (19:30)

The final moments in the life of Jesus focus on his radical obedience to his heavenly Father. Over and over again during the public ministry Jesus reminds us that he has come to do his Father's will. Typical of these reminders is the following:

"for I have come down from heaven, not to do my own will, but the will of him who sent me" (6:38). And the will of the Father is that Jesus is to reveal the truth about the hidden nature of God, namely, that divine power is forever in service of divine love. Jesus reveals this truth in his teaching but most of all in his example of perfect self-giving. That is why John tells us that, now that Jesus was about to die in total self-offering, he knew "that all was now finished" (19:28), that is, accomplished. He is now a perfect revelation of the divine love that he shares with his Father and the Spirit.

This obedience of Jesus to his heavenly Father is an obedience also to the Scriptures inspired by God. Thus, Jesus' dying fulfills all the aspirations of God's people. In particular, he fulfills those words of Psalm 69:21: "and for my thirst they gave me vinegar to drink." The offer of sour wine is in response to the cry of Jesus, "I am thirsty" (19:28), which is also reminiscent of Psalm 22:15, "my mouth is dried up like a potsherd, and my tongue sticks to my jaws . . ."—a passage which is just a few verses removed from the reference to dividing the afflicted man's garments (v. 18). In fulfilling these words of the Hebrew Scriptures, Jesus accomplishes all the purposes of God in human history.

Raymond Brown points out another pertinent text and notes the implications:

> Perhaps the most plausible symbolism is to connect the episode with xviii 11: "Am I not to drink the cup the Father has given me?" The cup was one of suffering and death, and now having finished his work, Jesus thirsts to drink the cup to the last drop, for only when he has tasted the bitter wine of death will his Father's will be fulfilled (*The Gospel according to John*, vol. 2, 930).

This scene corresponds to scene three, where we noted references to the priestly ministry of Jesus. This may explain why there is a mention here of the hyssop: "So they put a sponge full of the wine on a branch of hyssop and held it to his mouth" (19:29). The short and fragile hyssop branch would not have been suitable for that purpose but, on a symbolic level, it would evoke references to the hyssop branch, which was used to seal the covenant as the people were sprinkled with sacrificial blood. We read in the letter to the Hebrews:

> For when every commandment had been told to all the people by Moses in accordance with the law, he took the blood of calves and goats, with water and scarlet wool and hyssop, and sprinkled both the scroll itself and all the people, saying, "This is the blood of the covenant that God has ordained for you" (9:19-20).

Moses was the principal mediator between God and Israel and thus performed a priestly function in sealing the covenant with blood, thereby consecrating the people to God. For sharing the blood of the sacrificial victim was seen as a sharing of life itself and the supreme revelation of such sharing of God's life with us is the sacrifice of Jesus.

The Eucharist continues to make the Body and Blood of Jesus available to his followers. When received with a heart that is committed to loving service, this sacrament truly offers an intimate communion of life with Jesus and the Father, as John points out in 6:57: "Just as the living Father sent me, and I live because of the Father, so whoever eats me will live because of me." Sharing God's life is the fulfillment of the new covenant and the highest form of mystical union with the creator.

Having completed the work entrusted to him, Jesus "bowed his head and gave up his spirit" (19:30). On one level, this is a way of saying that Jesus has expired, but on a symbolic level it anticipates the giving of the Holy Spirit. Raymond Brown suggests as much when he notes that "John seems to play upon the idea that Jesus handed over the (Holy) Spirit to those at the foot of the cross, in particular, to his mother who symbolizes the Church or new people of God and to the Beloved Disciple who symbolizes the Christian" (*The Gospel according to John,* vol. 2, 931). We will see in chapters 5 and 6 that this Spirit is the Paraclete who cannot come until Jesus has died and who will continue to adapt the teaching of Jesus to the circumstances of all future ages.

Scene Six (19:31-37): *"One of the soldiers pierced his side with a spear, and at once blood and water came out"* (19:34)

Scene six corresponds to scene two in the chiastic arrangement. In John's passion narrative, the crucifixion of Jesus occurred on the afternoon before the Passover, which would have been the "day of great solemnity" mentioned in the first verse of this scene. In order to hasten the death of those crucified, so that the bodies could be removed before sundown, the soldiers proceed to break the legs of the victims, thereby causing them to slump and die quickly of asphyxiation. Such a scenario is quite plausible historically. But John does not relate this merely to satisfy our curiosity about "what really happened." He is far more interested in fulfilling Scripture and in seeing a powerful symbolism in the piercing of Jesus' side.

The first Scripture passage to be fulfilled is undoubtedly Exodus 12:46: "It (the Passover lamb) shall be eaten in one house . . . and you shall not break any of its bones." Neither shall the legs of Jesus be broken at his crucifixion. Thus, the sacrifice of Jesus is explicitly connected to that of the Passover lamb, which was offered to secure the liberation and safety of God's people as they fled from the bondage of Egypt. The loving sacrifice of Jesus now becomes the guarantee of freedom and safety for all peoples everywhere and until the end of time. To participate in this liberation, we must join him in the same kind of loving that reached its climax in his death for others.

An equally important symbolism is based on the piercing of Jesus' side and the resulting flow of blood and water. This is said to have fulfilled the biblical text, "They will look on the one whom they have pierced" (19:37). This refers undoubtedly to Zechariah 12:10:

> And I will pour out a spirit of compassion and supplication on the house of David and the inhabitants of Jerusalem, so that, when they look on the one whom they have pierced, they shall mourn for him as one mourns for an only child, and weep bitterly over him, as one weeps over a firstborn.

In this passage from Zechariah, it is not clear who the one pierced may be, but a likely possibility is the "Servant of Yahweh," a messianic figure featured in Isaiah (e.g., 53:5). When John refers to this text, he has in mind no doubt all those who witnessed the crucifixion and for whom this was the decisive moment in their lives. Indeed, one may include all those of any age who have recognized the significance of the death of Jesus and have responded, or failed to respond, to its challenge. Love inevitably leads to grieving as God allows our loved ones to be "pierced" by death, but the grieving will also be turned into joy.

All of this brings us back to the profound symbolism of the flow of blood and water from the pierced side of Jesus. The primary symbolism can be found in the reference of Jesus himself to the flow of water that will come from the heart of believers and which he then identifies as the Spirit:

> On the last day of the festival, the great day, while Jesus was standing there, he cried out, "Let anyone who is thirsty come to me, and let the one who believes in me drink. As the scripture has said, 'Out of the believer's heart shall flow rivers of living water.'" Now he said this about the Spirit, which believers in him were to receive . . . (7:37-39).

Now that Jesus has died, the era of the Spirit begins as John here anticipates the imminent coming of the Spirit at Pentecost.

The fact that both blood and water are said to have flowed from the side of Jesus is best explained by a text from 1 John: "This is the one who came by water and blood, Jesus Christ, not with the water only but with the water and the blood" (5:6). John the Baptist offered a baptism of water only, but Jesus told Nicodemus that one must be baptized in a new way that causes one to be "born of water and Spirit" (3:5). Now that Jesus has died, the blood also becomes part of the believer's baptismal participation in his experience.

The text from 1 John continues with a reference to the witnessing of the Spirit: "And the Spirit is the one that testifies, for the Spirit is the truth" (5:6). John seems to have this in mind when he adds a parenthetical statement about the testimony of an eyewitness: "He who saw this has testified so that you also may believe. His testimony is true, and he knows that he tells the truth" (19:35). We recall that Jesus told Pilate that he came into the world to testify to the truth (18:37). Now an eyewitness, who is undoubtedly the Beloved Disciple, testifies also to the truth, which is *both* the revelation of Jesus about the power of unselfish love *and* the exercise of that power in the love that culminates in his self-giving. The flow of blood and water from the heart cavity of Jesus' body symbolizes the generosity to which the Beloved Disciple bears witness.

This leads us to a secondary symbolism that refers to the Christian sacraments of baptism and Eucharist. These sacraments are the primary rites of Christian initiation and are therefore the principal ritual acts by which we are incorporated into the experience of Jesus, and especially into his death and resurrection. This happens, of course, only on condition that we live the meaning of baptism and Eucharist through the kind of loving that is expressed in the dying of Jesus.

We can see now how this scene corresponds to scene three where the priestly mediation of Jesus was portrayed. For the giving of the Spirit and the sacraments of baptism and Eucharist are all means by which the saving grace of the Father's love is offered to us through Jesus Christ. This priestly mediation is not restricted to the ordained ministry, however, but belongs to all who are baptized and who thereby participate in the continuing ministry of Jesus. Priestly ordination gives a special role to certain Christians but this does not exclude a general priesthood of all baptized Christians.

Scene Seven (19:38-42): *"And so . . . they laid Jesus there"* (19:42)

This scene stands in contrast to scene one, where Jesus is lifted up on the cross, just as here he is taken down from the cross and laid in a new tomb. The primary emphasis, however, is on the extraordinary care given to the dead body of Jesus.

We are told that Nicodemus "came, bringing a mixture of myrrh and aloes, weighing about a hundred pounds" (19:39). This surprising quantity of spices tells us that Jesus was prepared for burial in a way that befits the interment of a king. Raymond Brown sums it up well when he writes: "the theme that Jesus was buried as a king would fittingly conclude a Passion Narrative wherein Jesus is crowned and hailed as king during his trial and enthroned and publicly acclaimed as king on the cross" (*The Gospel according to John*, vol. 2, 960).

This then is the conclusion of the narrative of the crucifixion and death of Jesus which, while clearly similar to the Synoptics' accounts, nonetheless highlights those elements which are of primary interest to John. In the trial before Pilate, we see that the issue for John is the nature and exercise of power and that Jesus identifies the true source of power as the love of the Father made available now in Jesus. The crucifixion and death of Jesus, as the perfect exercise of his loving, reveals his true power and kingship hidden under the appearances of weakness and vulnerability. The resurrection will confirm in the most dramatic way the validity and availability of this divine power in our world.

4

Love Conquers All

In John's Gospel the story of the resurrection of Jesus is almost anticlimactic. The divinity of Jesus has already been displayed so that, even in the darkest moments of his passion, he seems to be in charge of what is happening. But it is nonetheless important to show how the power of Jesus' love conquered everything in the end. The fact that John devotes so much time to a discussion of the nature of that power of love simply alerts us to the fact that the readers of the Gospel, in John's day and ever since, must come to terms with the cost of love before they can savor its victory. We can readily identify with Jesus' suffering, whereas we can only anticipate Jesus' final victory over death. Nonetheless, John does give us an account of the resurrection of Jesus which is, once again, both similar to and quite different from the accounts found in the Synoptics. Mary Magdalene, for instance, plays a much more prominent role in John's resurrection story.

"He saw and believed" (20:8)

Mary Magdalene is the first to discover that the tomb of Jesus is empty, and her first thought is that someone has come during the night and removed the body. So she hurries to Peter and the "other disciple, the one whom Jesus loved . . ." (20:2), and tells them about her disturbing discovery. They both hurry to the tomb but the Beloved Disciple outruns Peter and arrives there first. In a profoundly symbolic gesture, he steps aside and allows Peter to enter the tomb ahead of him. This "body language" represents a clear recognition of Peter's traditional role as leader of the apostles. But it also reveals that the anonymous Beloved Disciple, by his deference to Peter, shows that he possesses the kind of humble, self-effacing love, which was the ideal taught by Jesus.

Raymond Brown has pointed out that Peter and the Beloved Disciple are contrasted more than once in the passion story of John and that, in each instance, the Beloved Disciple appears to be the more perfect follower of Jesus. Brown writes:

> In five of the six passages where he is mentioned, the Beloved Disciple is explicitly contrasted with Peter: in 13:23-26 the Beloved Disciple rests on Jesus' chest, while Peter has to signal to him for information; in 18:15-16 the Beloved Disciple can accompany Jesus into the high priest's palace, while Peter cannot enter without his help; in 20:2-10 the Beloved Disciple outruns Peter to the tomb, and only he is said to believe on the basis of what he sees there; in 21:7 the Beloved Disciple recognizes Jesus standing on the shore of the Sea of Tiberias and tells Peter who it is; in 21:20-23 when Peter jealously inquires about the Beloved Disciple's fate, he is told by Jesus, "Suppose I would like him to remain until I come, how does that concern you?" In a sixth passage (19:26-27), where the Beloved Disciple appears at the foot of the cross, the contrast is implicit: Peter is one of those who have scattered, abandoning Jesus (16:32) (*The Community of the Beloved Disciple*, 82–3).

Brown's insightful observation should not be interpreted as a questioning of the authority of Peter as leader of the apostles and of the Church. However, it is clear that John does want us to see in the Beloved Disciple a charismatic, mystical figure who most perfectly embodies that special kind of loving that is the heart of the truth that Jesus came to reveal. The relationship between Peter and the Beloved Disciple is very similar to that between the king and prophet in the Hebrew Scriptures. The king, blest by God, guarantees the structural and jurisdictional dimension of God's people, while the prophet, equally blest by God, represents the less structured, charismatic side of the community. Both are indispensable and they are meant to exist in a kind of healthy tension. Where there is only the king's order, there is danger of tyranny; where the prophet alone holds sway, there can be chaos! Through the experience of division and disunity revealed in the letters of John, the Johannine community will learn how important the structural dimension can be, but in the Gospel the primary concern is to emphasize the deep mystical dimension of Christian life. It is this mystical sensitivity that allows the Beloved Disciple to "see and believe" with an instinct that is unerring.

"I have seen the Lord" (20:18)

Mary Magdalene, after reporting her discovery of the open tomb to Peter and the Beloved Disciple, returns to the tomb and is weeping there. Finally, she looks into the tomb and discovers that two angels are there "sitting where the body of Jesus had been lying . . ." (20:12). The angels ask her why she is weeping and she replies, "They have taken away my Lord, and I do not know where they have laid him" (20:13). At that point, she turns around and sees a man standing nearby whom she does not recognize. She thinks he is the gardener and she asks him if he knows what has become of Jesus' body.

We recall that there are angels at the tomb of Jesus in the Synoptics' accounts also, but in that case they immediately announce that Jesus is risen from the dead (see Mark 16:5-6). John however wants this discovery to be made, not simply by announcing a fact of history, but in an experience of loving recognition: "Jesus said to her, 'Mary!'" (20:16). This name must have been spoken in such a loving way that she could have no doubt about the identity of her friend. She then replies in an equally personal way, for John takes the trouble to tell us that her *Rabbouni* was in Hebrew (Aramaic) to emphasize its familiar, intimate quality. Quite instinctively, Mary then embraces Jesus. But he asks her gently to let go of him. He has not really returned to her world, as if there had been no crucifixion and death. He belongs now to another world and he has appeared here only to let her know that he is alive and that all is well. When he has ascended to his Father and sent the Spirit, she will be able to embrace him in a new and much better way.

It is remarkable that John devotes so much attention to Mary Magdalene's encounter with Jesus in a rather short chapter on the resurrection. This merely serves to emphasize John's conviction that all revelation of divine presence happens primarily in a mystical experience of loving recognition rather than through an impersonal exchange of information. Therefore, when Mary Magdalene later tells the disciples, "I have seen the Lord" (20:18), she is enunciating the Johannine ideal of personal and mystical experience of God in human life. Mary Magdalene is afforded so much attention precisely because John sees in her a model for all Christians.

"As the Father has sent me, so I send you" (20:21)

On the evening of that day of resurrection, Jesus appears to the disciples huddled in fear behind locked doors. As they try to comprehend the meaning of his sudden appearance, he offers them a greeting, which dispels their fears and fills them with wonder and joy: "Peace be with you" (20:19). Though this was a common greeting at that time, it took on new meaning in the mouth of one who had died and now appeared to them alive and well. It is as if they now understand the meaning of peace for the first time. Indeed, this shalom/peace is not just the absence of conflict, which is what we commonly mean by peace, but a deep, serene confidence that laughs at fear and is full of hope.

We can only begin to imagine the relief and joyful surprise of the disciples as Jesus shows them the wounds in his hands and his side to assure them that it is indeed their beloved master who stands before them. It must surely be the ultimate understatement when John tells us, "Then the disciples rejoiced when they saw the Lord" (20:20).

Jesus repeats his greeting, "Peace be with you," and then gives them the most important mandate that any disciple can receive: "As the Father has sent me, so I send you" (20:21). This simple statement is almost a summary of John's whole Gospel, where he constantly speaks of his being sent by the Father. And the purpose of this mission is to reveal the love that the Father prizes more than anything else: "For God so loved the world that he gave his only Son . . ." (3:16).

Jesus himself, as the Word of God, embodies this love of the Father and manifests it for all to see—in his works of healing, in his words of wisdom, and, most of all, in his total self-sacrifice. Now the one sent by the Father sends his own disciples, of all times and places, to become themselves embodiments of the unselfish love that is in the heart of the Father and his Son. No doubt this mission includes the power to define faith and to organize the Church but, above and beyond all that, it means to love and to liberate, to heal and to comfort, to give one's very life so that others may share in the resurrection peace and joy.

"Receive the Holy Spirit" (20:22)

After Jesus assigns to the disciples (and to all of us) the mission of making his love present in the world, he offers the strength to carry out such a difficult task: "he breathed on them and said to them, 'Receive the Holy Spirit'" (20:22). This is like a new creation scene in which Jesus enlivens and empowers his followers much as the creator breathed life into the first human being (Gen 2:7). We will see in chapters 5 and 6 how John understands the influence of the Spirit on the disciples whom Jesus leaves behind.

Then Jesus singles out what is clearly the very first duty of his followers: "If you forgive the sins of any, they are forgiven them; if you retain the sins of any, they are retained" (20:23). This can only mean that one of the primary effects of true Christian love is the willingness to forgive others who may have hurt us in any way. This is an awesome responsibility and it cannot be restricted simply to the sacrament of reconciliation. Every one of us is offered the help of the Spirit so that we may have the courage to forgive and, if we do not do so, in some very real and tragic sense the healing will be thwarted.

Sometimes I think that the only question that we will be asked at the last judgment will be, quite simply, Did you let my people go? In other words, Was the overall effect of your presence in the world to liberate or to hold in bondage? Were you a Moses, friend of God, or a pharaoh, holding others in slavery? Forgiveness can be very difficult but that is precisely why Jesus sends his powerful Spirit to assist us.

"Thomas answered him, 'My Lord and my God'" (20:28)

It is somewhat surprising to see Thomas featured so prominently in the relatively brief Johannine account of the post-resurrection appearances of Jesus. Thomas has cameo roles earlier in the Gospel where he is identified as the "twin" and where he makes an abrupt and rather rash suggestion that he and the other disciples should simply go up to Jerusalem and die with Jesus (11:16). And it is he who asks Jesus in what sense he is the way to salvation (14:5). He merits a mention also in chapter 21, where he is again identified as the "twin" (v. 2).

Thomas may in fact have been a twin since his name means "twin" in Aramaic. It is more likely, however, that Thomas was called a twin because he had a striking physical resemblance to Jesus. In that case, his reluctance to believe the report that Jesus had been seen alive would be John's way of emphasizing that no merely human advantage counts for anything in one's relationship with the Lord. The only thing that really matters is a living, dynamic faith which is what finally enlightens Thomas and enables him to cry out, "My Lord and my God" (20:28). Only at this moment does he really begin to "look like" Jesus. Once again, John insists on an ideal of personal and mystical union with Jesus.

"That disciple whom Jesus loved said to Peter, 'It is the Lord!'" (21:7)

Although chapter 21 is generally considered an epilogue to the Gospel of John, it does continue to discuss the consequences of the resurrection. Thus, there is an appearance of Jesus on the shore of the Sea of Tiberias in Galilee. Jesus appears to several of the disciples while they are fishing and intervenes to produce an extraordinary catch of fish.

John does not explain how the disciples could have returned to their former way of life after having received the Spirit in Jerusalem. One must remember, however, that the real concern of John is theology rather than history. In terms of his theology, the climax of the story occurs when the Beloved Disciple recognizes Jesus and identifies him for Peter: "That disciple whom Jesus loved said to Peter, 'It is the Lord!'" (21:7). Once again, this does not mean that he is challenging Peter's leadership role; it is intended merely to highlight the special mystical intuition of the Beloved Disciple.

The clear implication of all this is that administrative leaders in the Church, on all levels, should pay attention to the insights of those who are mystically attuned to the ways of the Spirit. Or better perhaps, they should pay attention to the mystical side of their own personalities. Logic has its value but it must also make room for spiritual intuition.

Jesus then invites the disciples to join him for breakfast. At that point, "Jesus came and took the bread and gave it to them, and did the same with the fish" (21:13). All through John's Gospel, Jesus is portrayed as the one who offers us life. At the end of chapter 20, we read: "these (words) are written so that you may come to believe that Jesus is the Messiah, the Son of God, and that through believing *you may have life* in his name" (20:31, emphasis added). An essential element in this life-giving mission of Jesus is nourishment. We will see this especially in the discourse where Jesus identifies himself as "the bread of life" (6:35). For readers of John's Gospel at the end of the first century (and ever since), this action of Jesus is recognized as a foreshadowing of their experience of life-giving Eucharist.

"Simon son of John, do you love me more than these?" (21:15)

When Jesus questions Peter three times about his love for the Master, he is providing him with an opportunity to reverse the threefold denial made during those awful days of the passion. This is hard for Peter, and he shows his anguish: "Peter felt hurt because he said to him the third time, 'Do you love me?' And he said to him, 'Lord, you know everything; you know that I love you'" (21:17). The implication is that Peter must accept this humbling experience to make amends for his previous infidelity.

All in all, however, the scene is very favorable to Peter whose role as chief shepherd in the Church is affirmed three times by Jesus. The lambs and the sheep that Peter is to nurture are all of the faithful, including the other disciples. Thus, the primacy of Peter is affirmed here in the clearest terms, even if the Beloved Disciple is the obvious favorite of John's Gospel.

Peter will also have the privilege of joining his beloved master in the ultimate witness of love by giving up his life. For Jesus says to him,

> Very truly, I tell you, when you were younger, you used to fasten your own belt and to go wherever you wished. But when you grow old, you will stretch out your hands, and someone else will fasten a belt around you and take you where you do not wish to go (21:18).

The author goes on to tell us that this foreshadowed Peter's death which would be his last act of love and generosity. As a disciple of Jesus, he is pledged to be consistently unselfish, and that is a gradual dying long before death actually arrives.

In a similar manner, we too die a little every time we act unselfishly, and we thereby prepare ourselves for the final offering. All this is surely implied when Jesus said to Peter, "Follow me" (21:19). Just as the power of Jesus' love was never more clearly evident than when he stood bound before Pilate, so also the love of his followers will be invincible when it least appears to be so. In that sense a feeble octogenarian filled with love is far more powerful than a robust youngster without much concern for others!

John continues to reflect upon the implications of the resurrection of Jesus in the "farewell discourses" (13:31–17:26) which we will now consider in chapters 5 to 6. It was only through years of striving to live by the wisdom of Jesus that the community of John was able to discover the real meaning of his death and resurrection. In this effort, they were assisted powerfully by the Spirit of Jesus, present and active in their midst. The lengthy discourse of Jesus which precedes the passion story is in fact a series of reflections on what happened *after* the resurrection of Jesus as the community struggled to understand the implications of that momentous event for their daily lives. In this effort, they were assisted by the Paraclete/Spirit, who inspired them to trust the power of unselfishness in a world that prizes other kinds of power.

These discourses are addressed to all of us as well. Being attentive and obedient to the Spirit among us is the only way to discover who Jesus really is and how we can gradually come to live and love in him and thereby to become participants in his divine life. In a word, these discourses lead us into a deeper appreciation of that truth which became incarnate in Jesus and which enables us to make the most of this wonderful opportunity we call human life.

5

Love One Another

It is a little surprising to find in John's Gospel that, after the Last Supper and before the arrest of Jesus, a lengthy "farewell discourse" is inserted. It begins with 13:31 and does not end until 17:26. There seems to be good reason to divide this section into three discourses with the divisions occurring at the end of chapters 14 and 16. As noted before, it seems appropriate to discuss these words of Jesus *after* the passion story because they are in fact a very personal and mystical exploration of the implications of the death and resurrection of Jesus for his followers. As these disciples struggled through persecution and rejection, they recalled words spoken by Jesus that will now help them to understand better all the implications of the death and resurrection of their Master.

We see a very similar phenomenon in the case of the book of Deuteronomy, which claimed to be the final instructions of Moses to assist the Israelites in their future existence in Canaan, but which was in fact written long after that had happened. They drew upon earlier teachings of Moses in order to find guidance for their lives in this new land. The words of

Jesus, therefore, like those of Moses, are thought to carry more weight when presented as their last instructions before death.

"Love one another" (13:34)

Judas has just left the little group to join the encircling darkness (13:30). Jesus tells his remaining disciples that the end is near but he does so in mystical language: "Now the Son of Man has been glorified, and God has been glorified in him" (13:31). In biblical usage the word "glory" has a special meaning. It signifies any sense-perceptible manifestation of God's presence in our world. Thus, for example, the luminous cloud that accompanied the Israelites after they left Egypt is called "the glory of the Lord" (Exod 16:10) because it represented God's visible presence with his people. When Jesus says that he has now been glorified, he means that the die has been cast and that the ultimate meaning and purpose of his life will soon be made clear. This will happen when he is lifted up in crucifixion as the perfect sign of his, and his Father's, love for us. Since the love of Jesus is manifested most clearly in his dying for us, the glorification of Jesus in John's Gospel always refers to his crucifixion rather than to his resurrection.

Jesus then declares the meaning *for us* of his final act of loving sacrifice: "I give you a new commandment, that you love one another. Just as I have loved you, you also should love one another" (13:34). This is called a new commandment because, although God's love for us has been previously manifested in many ways, no one could dream that it would reach the point where the Son of God would die for us. At first glance, it appears that Jesus is asking us to imitate his loving by our love for one another. Of course, his unselfish loving is indeed a model for us but, as Raymond Brown points out, much more than that is intended here. He writes: "love is more than a commandment; it is a gift" (*The Gospel according to John*, vol. 2, 612). In other words, it is a commandment that we would never be able to observe were it not for the fact that we have been created to share the very life of God, which is love. We must want to love unselfishly but the ability to do so will come from God's goodness.

This cooperation between our desire and God's gift of life is so important that it may help to note an example, which illustrates the dynamics involved. The miracle of the multiplication of loaves and fishes is so important for the gospel tradition that it is found in all four Gospels. In each case, the size of the hungry crowd is noted and Jesus asks the disciples to feed them. The disciples protest that what he asks of them is clearly impossible, and we even note an element of hurt in their responses. In John's version, "Philip answered him, 'Six months' wages would not buy enough bread for each of them to get a little'" (6:7). Nonetheless, Jesus instructs them to distribute what little they have and, much to their surprise, there is not only enough to feed all the hungry people but baskets-full of fragments are left over. The obvious lesson is that we must trust God's goodness and understand that God enables us to initiate good works even if our resources seem meager, for the Lord will continue to be with us and will make our efforts amazingly fruitful.

"I am the way, and the truth, and the life" (14:6)

In chapter 14 Jesus begins by consoling the disciples with the reminder that he will not forget them after his departure. In fact, he will provide many dwelling places for them in his Father's house. The words are a model of tender concern: "And if I go and prepare a place for you, I will come again and will take you to myself, so that where I am, there you may be also" (14:3). However, when he adds that the disciples already know how to reach this wonderful homeland, Thomas objects, pointing out that they know neither the place where he is going nor how to get there.

"Jesus said to him, 'I am the way, and the truth, and the life. No one comes to the Father except through me'" (14:6). Jesus is going to his Father—that loving One—whose presence defines the meaning of home, so that all the homes we have ever known pale by comparison. And the way to this place of love and harmony is well known; it is Jesus himself. However, we should note, with Raymond Brown, that Jesus is not saying here that his mission can be summed up in three distinct realities: way, truth, and life. Rather, he is the only *way* to salvation because he teaches the only valid *truth* and the proof of this is that he leads his followers to the only *life* that truly deserves the name (see *The Gospel according to John*, vol. 2, 630–1).

This truth is, of course, the same truth for which Jesus came into the world, as we saw in his dialogue with Pilate. It is the critical revelation that the very purpose of our existence is to love unselfishly and that we will fulfill that purpose only if we use what freedom we have to love as unselfishly as we possibly can. Moreover, Jesus is not the way simply because he tells us about it but, far more importantly, because his life is an embodiment of this unselfishness. Accordingly, to follow his way means to become unselfish in and with him.

"Whoever has seen me has seen the Father" (14:9)

In John's Gospel the Father is that wonderfully transcendent and hidden God of biblical tradition. Even Moses, whom God regarded as a dear friend, was not allowed to look upon the face of this God (Exod 33:20). And this is the God that Jesus came to reveal to us according to John's Prologue: "No one has ever seen God. It is God the only Son, who is close to the Father's heart, who has made him known" (1:18). When Jesus tells his disciples that they know the Father and have seen him, it is not surprising that Philip should conclude that this wonderful possibility still lies in the future: "Lord, show us the Father, and we will be satisfied" (14:8). This provides Jesus with another opportunity to stress something that he proclaims throughout the Gospel of John.

"Have I been with you all this time, Philip, and you still do not know me? *Whoever has seen me has seen the Father*" (14:9, emphasis added). In the biblical tradition prior to Jesus, God was known primarily for his power and, though the Israelites were grateful for that power when it was exercised in their favor, they were also easily frightened by God's mysterious nature and by his unpredictability. Jesus came to reveal the most hidden and mysterious part of God's nature, which is his infinite capacity for loving. Moreover, Jesus does not merely state this as a fact but he claims to have experienced that love as the eternal Word and now reveals what he himself has heard in his position "close to the Father's heart" (1:18), where he can, in a sense, hear the very heartbeat of the Father.

This union between Father and divine Son is so intimate that Jesus can say simply that seeing him is the same as seeing the Father. And what one sees is not just the miraculous power of Jesus exercised for a short time in Galilee but that loving trust in his Father's goodness that carried him through terrible darkness and suffering as he gave his life for us. In a word, the Father cherishes us just as much as Jesus does for there is an unbreakable bond between them: "Believe me that I am in the Father and the Father is in me" (14:11).

Jesus then makes a promise that could scarcely be believed if it were not from his own lips: "Very truly, I tell you, the one who believes in me will also do the works that I do and, in fact, will do greater works than these, because I am going to the Father" (14:12). If we enter by faith into that flow of life between Father and Son, we will be empowered to perform the very works of loving and healing that characterized the life of Jesus. In fact, we will be able to do even greater works because Jesus will be acting through us to carry on the work of salvation. The all-powerful love of Jesus, experienced through faith, will join our own feeble loving to make it wonderfully fruitful.

It is consoling to know that even the most difficult loving and serving can be accomplished with the help of Jesus. And we should have no doubt about that in view of his explicit promise to be with us in any good work that we undertake. "I will do whatever you ask in my name, so that the Father may be glorified in the Son. If in my name you ask me for anything, I will do it" (14:13-14). The Father is glorified when his hidden goodness is revealed, as it is when we do good deeds because of the power of Jesus within us.

"This is the Spirit of truth" (14:17)

John's Gospel is about the revelation of ultimate truth. We have seen that Jesus told Pilate, at a moment of truth in his own life, that he had come into the world to bear witness to the truth (18:37). As noted earlier, this truth is the revelation of the radical and immense goodness of the Father, experienced by Jesus and manifested in his self-giving for others. We are invited to participate in this truth, not simply by hearing about it, but by *experiencing* the love of the Father and thus becoming one with Jesus in the most important experience of his life. At this point in his first farewell discourse, Jesus introduces the Holy Spirit, the third person in the Trinity, and announces the unique role of this Spirit in regard to that truth which is at the center of his mission.

"If you love me, you will keep my commandments. And I will ask the Father, and he will give you another Advocate, to be with you forever. This is the Spirit of truth . . ." (14:15-17). Keeping Jesus' commandments means trusting his words and striving to love as he did. When that condition is fulfilled, it will be possible to receive "another Advocate" who will take the place of Jesus, as we will soon see, and will become the constant and permanent companion of the believer. (It is possible to translate this passage in a different way, namely, "he will give you another one, an Advocate." However, since Jesus is also called an "advocate" in 1 John 2:1, it seems best to conclude that Jesus refers to the Spirit as the other Advocate.)

What does John mean when he calls the Holy Spirit our "Advocate"? Other translations of the Greek word *paracletos* have seen suggested, such as, "Counselor," "Consoler," or "Sponsor," and some even abandon the search for an appropriate English word and call him simply the "Paraclete." However, since the Greek word means literally "one called to the side of another," the name "Advocate," which has the same meaning in its Latin root, would seem to be preferable. This word suggests, therefore, that the Spirit is one who stands with us believers to defend us against enemies or to prosecute others who may be infringing on our rights. Such a forensic understanding would be most appropriate in John's Gospel where there is so much talk about judgment (e.g., 3:19).

This divine Advocate is called "the Spirit of truth" because it is the Spirit's task to assist the believer in discovering all the implications of the profound truth revealed by Jesus. John goes on to say that "the world cannot receive" this Spirit of truth (14:17), and the reason is that the worldly ones have chosen to trust the false promise that selfishness will bring success and happiness. They can never welcome one who will challenge that very attractive conviction. It will be altogether different, however, for believers: "You know him, because he abides with you, and he will be in you" (14:17). In other words, those who participate in the loving of Jesus will instinctively recognize and embrace the presence of this Spirit, who is sent by Jesus and comes from the Father. Once again, John places the emphasis, not on intellectual comprehension or theological correctness, but on mystical experience.

"Because I live, you also will live" (14:19)

Life is a very precious gift, and we cling to it, sometimes desperately. But the life we try to protect is ephemeral and was never meant to last. We may be surprised to discover that we are mortal, but it is consoling to know that God is not surprised that we should die; therefore it can hardly be such a bad thing. Jesus tells his disciples that his going away through death will separate him from the world, which risks missing its chance to know him, but he will remain alive for those who trust his words and who make him the center of their lives. Death cannot come between Jesus and his friends. This new life is not the passing life of our bodily existence but the true and lasting life of loving union with Jesus and the Father. "On that day you will know that I am in my Father, and you in me, and I in you" (14:20). Jesus is referring to the day of his death but what he says is true for the day of our death too. The believer will know by then that real life is to be in loving union with Jesus and that such life cannot be touched by death.

Once again, John emphasizes the importance of experience. It is desirable to know the right words and to perform the right rituals because they help to protect us from false religious experience, but it is the mystical experience of union with God in Jesus that is essential. All the right words and right rituals will be worse than useless if they are thought to be sufficient in themselves. Mystical experience is an unmediated contact with God. Ritual or verbal mediums are important, but they are only mediums. Jesus is certainly demanding more than correct doctrine or right ritual when he says: "Those who love me will keep my word, and my Father will love them, and we will come to them and make our home with them" (14:23). Keeping his word means to love as he loves—indeed, loving with his loving.

"The Holy Spirit . . . will teach you everything" (14:26)

During his public ministry Jesus taught his disciples many things, but they had not been able to understand much of what he said. For the essence of his teaching was revealed in the event of his death and resurrection, and this event still lay in the future for them. What the Holy Spirit will teach them concerns the tremendous implications of the dying and rising of their Savior. Nothing that Jesus said or did can be really understood apart from this climax to his career.

Once again it is the Advocate, now explicitly identified as the Holy Spirit, who will continue and deepen the teaching of Jesus. In this way the Spirit will defend them against the insidious but attractive suggestion that human happiness can come from any other source than unselfish loving. Such temptations are deceitful and misleading but they are so attractive that we would never be able to resist them without the aid of the Spirit. Accordingly, Jesus promises that "the Advocate, the Holy Spirit, whom the Father will send in my name, will teach you everything, and remind you of all that I have said to you" (14:26).

When John says that the Spirit will explain and expand on the teaching of Jesus, we must not imagine that he means that the Spirit will simply add more pages to the treatise on christology. The most important contribution of the Spirit will be to show us how to experience Jesus in a world that is so different from the world that he knew. Sometimes we say to ourselves, "I wonder what Jesus would do if he were in my situation." Since it is almost impossible to imagine what a person living in first-century Palestine would do in twenty-first-century America, we are very likely to conclude that Jesus would probably do exactly what we had already planned to do. Such reasoning can be very dangerous. But it is precisely at such a time that the Spirit can come to our aid and translate, as it were, the teaching of Jesus into the idiom of our world.

The implications of this become clearer when we consider several possible examples. It is obvious that Jesus never knew experientially what being an old person would be like. Yet there are many old people who very much want to experience old age in accordance with the wisdom of Jesus. The Spirit makes that possible. The same can be said for living the wisdom of Jesus as a rich person, or as a politician, or even as a professor of Scripture! In all such situations, far removed from the world of Jesus, the Spirit will tell us how to live by his wisdom. Moreover, it should be obvious that this recognition is not on the level of rational thought but on the deepest level of personal and mystical experience.

The effect of this identity with Jesus in all aspects of our lives will be a profound sense of confidence and peace. This surely must be what Jesus means when he continues: "Peace I leave with you; my peace I give to you. I do not give to you as the world gives. Do not let your hearts be troubled, and do not let them be afraid" (14:27). The world, consisting of those who do not know Jesus, may be able to provide occasionally a superficial sense of tranquillity—a kind of vacation experience—but only knowing and loving Jesus can bring a deep, constant peace that stays with us even when we are facing the most difficult challenges in life.

Jesus then warns the disciples that there will be difficult times ahead. "I will no longer talk much with you, for the ruler of this world is coming. He has no power over me; but I do as the Father has commanded me, so that the world may know that I love the Father" (14:30-31). The ruler or prince of this world is, of course, Satan, the "father of lies" (8:44), because he spreads the insidious falsehood that only selfishness pays off. He has powerful allies in this world and they will make Jesus die for the sake of his truth. The Father permits this because the self-giving of Jesus is the ultimate sign and proof of the truth that he teaches, and it also sets the stage for the resurrection which vindicates forever the wisdom of Jesus. This ultimate self-sacrifice of Jesus in obedience to the Father brings about a confrontation with Satan and guarantees his defeat.

At the end of chapter 14, Jesus gives his disciples a strange and unexpected exhortation: "Rise, let us be on our way" (14:31). These words, at their face value, seem to end the discourse and to set in motion some other happening, perhaps the passion event itself. But that is not what happens, for the discourse continues and the passion event is still three chapters away. Scholars have been accustomed to see here a kind of editorial lapse. They think that the final editor of the Gospel, in splicing together various sources, simply overlooked this statement which was in the tradition but which makes no sense in the present form of John's Gospel.

L. William Countryman, however, does not think this is an editorial lapse:

> I would suggest that it is not absent-mindedness that allowed the words to stand, but rather their structural usefulness and

their susceptibility to a mystical reading. Structurally, they mark the division between the two discourses, which would otherwise be hard to catch. This division is important for the reader precisely because the second discourse will rework material from the first and the reader needs a sense of a new beginning in order not to become disoriented. Mystically, the words can be read as an announcement that Jesus is about to move to a new level of speech (*The Mystical Way in the Fourth Gospel,* 2nd ed., 105).

I think this is a very insightful observation because it suggests that John will now move on to discuss in an even more profound and personal way the meaning of Jesus in the lives of us Christians. We shall see in the next discourse that this is exactly what happens.

6

Abide in Me as I Abide in You

I have noted that John signals a transition with the words of Jesus: "Rise, let us be on our way" (14:31). This is not to be understood, however, in a "Western," logical sense where we might expect a further development of earlier themes. Rather, we should look for a further contemplative reflection with even more daring images of how the believer relates to Jesus and the Father and the Spirit and how this affects our relationship to the world in which we live.

"I am the vine, you are the branches" (15:5)

Jesus was a native of Palestine where everyone knew about vineyards. He had often seen the thick vine-stocks with their roots deep in the soil and the branches or vines that radiated from that vine-stock. The sap or juice of life came through the vine-stock, and flowed into the branches. As long as the vines remained attached firmly to the vine-stock, they flourished in a profusion of leaves and grapes. But when that "life-blood" was cut off, they quickly withered and died.

Raymond Brown has noted the new dimension that this imagery brings to Jesus' discussion of his relationship with his disciples. He writes: "Hitherto the metaphors that concern the receiving of Jesus' gift of life have involved external actions: one has had to drink the water or eat the bread to have life." (Brown is referring, of course, to the "living" water offered to the Samaritan woman in chapter 4 and to the bread of life in chapter 6). He continues: "The imagery . . . of the vine is more intimate . . . one must remain in Jesus as a branch remains on a vine in order to have life" (*The Gospel according to John,* vol. 2, 672).

There are superficial ways of believing that accept all the doctrines about Jesus while avoiding a real personal commitment of faith. One cannot be united with Jesus as a branch is joined to the life-giving vine-stock without the actual experience of shared life and love. In this way, one begins to live with the life of Jesus and to love with his love. This life-giving love comes from the Father, whom Jesus calls the "vine-grower" (15:1), because he has "tended" the vine-stock by guiding Jesus to his final loving sacrifice for us.

When the Father "planted" the vine-stock of Jesus in our world, it was for the purpose of enabling us to attach ourselves to that source of life and to become fruitful in loving service. But the Father, as a wise vine-grower, knows that the fruitfulness of the vines will require careful pruning also. Anyone who is acquainted with viniculture will recognize immediately that vines allowed to grow unchecked will produce smaller and smaller grapes as the vines gradually return to their wild state. Likewise, anyone who has attempted to prune grapes will know how much discipline is required to cut away rich growth which seems so promising but which is more than the vine-stock can support. It has been said that the only mistake that can be made in pruning is to leave too much of the vine.

However, if pruning is difficult for the one who prunes, it is even more painful for the vine. In the analogy used by Jesus, the painful pruning of the believers attached to him represents the suffering that comes from loving unselfishly. For this will mean letting go of cherished plans for the sake of others. It will also mean abandoning false goals and dangerous illusions as love leads us to see the real opportunities in our lives. In this real life we will frequently need to trust the goodness of God in situations where God seems to have abandoned us. Sharing in the love of Christ means sharing also in his sacrifice. But the Father knows what is best for us and so "Every branch that bears fruit he prunes to make it bear more fruit" (15:2).

"Abide in me as I abide in you" (15:4)

One of John's favorite words is the Greek verb *meno*, which is usually translated as "abide" or "remain" or "continue." He uses this word more than all the other New Testament writers together and it is one of the richest words in his theological vocabulary. When he uses this word in reference to a person, it suggests a deeply personal and constant union. It would thus be contrasted with a contact that may be intense but which soon fades and has no lasting effect. To abide in Jesus is to be attached to him in such a way that life would seem impossible without him. "Abide in me as I abide in you. Just as the branch cannot bear fruit by itself unless it abides in the vine, neither can you unless you abide in me" (15:4). To be detached from Jesus is to live a shadow life that has no real meaning and that benefits no one in a permanent way. It is a waste of precious time.

Such abiding in Jesus does not mean, however, that one withdraws from life and thinks only of one's private relationship with him. For abiding in Jesus means living in his love which, being radically unselfish, reaches out to embrace all who are more needy than oneself. Jesus goes with us into the world and enables us to produce the lasting fruit of a loving, caring presence there.

Where one's deeds are not motivated by this kind of loving concern, one may indeed erect monuments to pride and ambition, but they are houses of cards that will soon collapse. "Those who abide in me and I in them bear much fruit, because apart from me you can do nothing. Whoever does not abide in me is thrown away like a branch and withers; such branches are gathered, thrown into the fire, and burned" (15:5-6). The apparently modest accomplishments that result from loving as Jesus does will remain and will never be forgotten.

"That your joy may be complete" (15:11)

Joy is a gift in life that is as elusive as it is precious. We cherish the moments when we are caught up in the experience of real joy. And we wonder how we can hold on to such moments, or how we can be sure that they will return. We are tempted to think that this will happen if we have our wishes fulfilled or can extend a moment of pleasure. Jesus tells us that real joy, like his resurrection, comes only after the suffering that accompanies unselfish loving. "If you keep my commandments, you will abide in my love, just as I have kept my Father's commandments and abide in his love" (15:10). The Father asked Jesus to be a model of real love, and that cost him dearly, but it meant abiding in the Father's love and that could only end in glorious resurrection. The same is true for us also.

There is a beautiful passage in the letter to the Hebrews that resonates with the same wisdom:

> . . . and let us run with perseverance the race that is set before us, looking to Jesus the pioneer and perfecter of our faith, who for the sake of the joy that was set before him endured the cross, disregarding its shame, and has taken his seat at the right hand of the throne of God (12:1-2).

Jesus has gone before us and has blazed the trail for us. He has endured the pain that real loving brings by keeping his eyes fixed on the "joy that was set before him"—a joy that is at the heart of the utterly trustworthy promise of his heavenly Father.

Joy may indeed seem to be elusive but only if we look in the wrong places for it. Those who dare to love as Jesus did, who are free enough to seek the happiness of others rather than just their own, will enter into his joy. This is the only perfect joy, and it will not prove to be a will-o'-the-wisp that merely tantalizes us. It will be full to overflowing and will last forever. We could never believe this if Jesus himself had not told us so. "I have said these things to you so that my joy may be in you, and that your joy may be complete" (15:11). Jesus offers us the wisdom that makes joy our partner in life, no matter what hardships may come our way.

"I have called you friends" (15:15)

These words of Jesus, perhaps more than any others, show us how this second discourse takes us to a new level in our personal experience of God in Jesus. The great Moses was said to be God's friend (Exod 33:11), but this would seem to be an ideal far beyond the aspirations of most of us. Yet Jesus does not hesitate to offer friendship to all of us. And he does what good friends always do—he shares his best gifts with us: "I have called you friends, because I have made known to you everything that I have heard from my Father" (15:15). Jesus offers us the key to his Father's treasure house and invites us to enter with him and to make the most of the riches found there. This is, of course, a treasure house of infinite love and Jesus says that he makes *all* of it available to us. To know that experientially is to have no more fear and to enjoy a peace beyond imagining. This is that truth for which the eternal Word became incarnate and which offers true freedom and fulfillment.

This is a free gift from Jesus. Fortunately, he does not ask whether we deserve it. "You did not choose me but I chose you" (15:16). And since it is the infinite love of his Father that Jesus offers us, he assures us that we need only ask that good Father for whatever we need and "the Father will give you whatever you ask him in my name" (15:16). And what we will always need to ask of the Father is that we may come to realize how much he loves us so that, in the resulting freedom, we may have the courage and strength to love one another. When we learn to do that we will experience the liberating friendship of Jesus. We will no longer be servants who often obey out of fear or for recompense; we will instead be ready and eager for whatever God may ask of us.

"If the world hates you" (15:18)

Jesus now alerts his followers to the danger of a naive optimism. What he has taught them about the need to love unselfishly will not be received gladly by those who put their faith in power and control. Jesus knows this because he has already experienced it in his ministry: "If the world hates you, be aware that it hated me before it hated you" (15:18).

In John's Gospel the world was created good. In fact, "God so loved the world, that he gave his only Son" (3:16). But this world may refuse to accept and follow that Son with his message of selfless love. It is only at that point that the world becomes the enemy of Jesus. One notes a change in the meaning of "world" in the development of the Fourth Gospel. At first it appears to be neutral but later in the Gospel it is portrayed as evil because most of the world does in fact resist the message of Jesus. At that point, the followers of Jesus are said to be called out of the world: "Because you do not belong to the world, but I have chosen you out of the world—therefore the world hates you" (15:19).

The world hates the disciples for the same reason that it hates Jesus, because both of them espouse an interpretation of human life that is a standing condemnation of the world's view of things. The world says: "Get as much freedom and power as you can and use it to dominate and control for that is the only way to happiness." Jesus and his disciples say: "Accept the gift of freedom and use it to empower others through loving service for that is the only path to happiness." Even those who follow the world's philosophy must at least suspect that Jesus may be right. They need to show, therefore, that he is a misguided idealist and they need to persecute those whose lives demonstrate that Jesus is in fact the only true realist. Unfortunately, this issue is often resolved only at the end and in the meantime the disciples of Jesus must live in trust and hope.

"*Whoever hates me hates my Father also*" (15:23)

Throughout the Gospel of John, Jesus is intent on establishing an unbreakable bond between himself and the hidden God whom he knows as loving Father. The followers of Jesus trust this bond and are convinced that Jesus is the way to the Father and to fulfillment in a wonderful homeland. Others however claim that Jesus cannot be the way because he is too careless about observing the religious laws of his day. Still others reject him because he threatens their power base by questioning the religious structures represented by the temple. These religious authorities also claim to be in touch with God, but they cannot accept Jesus as God's true prophet. They are especially hostile toward the Johannine community because of their claims about the divine nature of Jesus, which in the eyes of these Jewish compatriots amounts to blasphemy. This is a passionate issue and it leads to harsh words on both sides.

If Jesus had not worked miracles of mercy to support his claim, his opponents might have been excused. But his miraculous power was a divine stamp of approval on him and clearly validated his claim to be God's prophet. "If I had not done among them the works that no one else did, they would not have sin. But now they have seen and hated both me and my Father" (15:24). For the Johannine community, this resistance is incomprehensible. They know what Jesus means to them and they cannot understand how anyone could reject his offer of salvation. But neither do they understand how easily one can become wedded to familiar religious structures that give a certain security without being too demanding. Thus we note in these words of Jesus, which also reflect the feelings of the community, an element of sadness that what is so good should be so easily rejected.

Once again we note how two levels of meaning are discernible in the text as the experiences of the Johannine community in the 70s and 80s are attributed to Jesus during his ministry in the late 20s. This is no doubt due in part to the intense sense of mystical union between them and Jesus, so that his presence among them is experienced as a more powerful reality than the decades of history which separate them. When Jesus is shown warning them, therefore, about future opposition and hatred, it is not just a prediction of what may be but a statement of what has been and is now. And when Jesus says, "they will put you out of the synagogues" (16:2), his words do not apply to his historical ministry when Jesus himself was welcomed in the synagogue (Luke 4:16ff.), but rather reflect the condition of the Johannine community perhaps fifty years later. From the perspective of this community, Jesus truly lives with them and suffers with them.

"When the Advocate comes" (15:26)

John's reference to the coming of the promised Advocate, who is called "the Spirit of truth" (15:26), takes on special meaning after the warnings of Jesus about coming controversy and opposition. It is said that the Advocate "comes from the Father" and that "he will testify on my behalf" (15:26). The Johannine community must have felt small and vulnerable in comparison to the hostile public opinion arrayed against them. It is important then that they have the assurance that God's powerful Advocate-Spirit stands with them to reassure them about the validity of their cause. This Spirit, like Jesus, comes from the Father and can bear witness therefore to that bond which ties Jesus to the Father and guarantees that his revolutionary message is indeed divinely inspired and completely trustworthy.

This Advocate is called the Spirit of truth because he will uphold that truth for which Jesus came into the world (18:37) and which he proclaimed at the climactic moment of his final sacrifice. This truth is about the Father's love for us—a love so intense that it can liberate us from even the most binding addictions and most paralyzing fears so that we may respond joyfully and gratefully to the ultimate Good News. If the Pharisees could hear this truth, they would be liberated from their addiction to scrupulous legal observance, just as the religious authorities would also be freed from inadequate and humanly contrived religious structures. Their modern counterparts can also be liberated by the Spirit of truth so that they too may see that laws are very helpful when subordinated to love and that ecclesiastical structures must also be recognized as no more than a means to a spiritual end of loving service.

"Sorrow has filled your hearts" (16:6)

It is impossible for us to imagine how confused and disappointed the disciples must have been in their relationship with Jesus. I have often thought that, if we should some day come upon a page from the diary of Peter, most entries would contain the same sad line, "He didn't make any sense today either!" We know how distraught they all were when he predicted that "the Son of Man must undergo great suffering . . ." (Mark 8:31) and how Peter took him aside to remonstrate with him only to be severely rebuked. All this is reflected in the frequent references in John's Gospel to his imminent departure from them: "now I am going to him who sent me . . . because I have said these things to you, sorrow has filled your hearts" (16:5-6).

Parting is surely one of the most painful experiences of human life. Whether it is a child leaving home or a loved one going far away or the final separation of death, it occurs so often that we find grief and sorrow to be never far from our daily experience. Life seems to be a constant round of hellos and good-byes and, as we grow older, the good-byes begin to overtake and pass the hellos. This would be a truly tragic situation if we did not have the faith conviction that the resurrection of Jesus guarantees that all our hellos will be gathered up and claim victory in the end. And this is exactly what Jesus implies when he tells them that his going away will mean that the Advocate-Spirit will come to assure them of that final victory of hello over good-bye, of happy greeting over sad farewell.

In God's loving plan, the victory was never meant to take place here, much as we would like that to happen. Thus we must endure the painful twinges that are inevitable for those who are on a journey. Legitimate but provisional attachments must give way to permit the only attachment that will never need to be broken—our attachment to the Father in Jesus and the Spirit. We will know then that this world, though a wonderful place to visit, was never meant to be our real home. The Spirit helps us to understand this as he creates in us a kind of homesickness—an aching void—that can never be filled with anything less than God. St. Paul understood this perfectly when he wrote that in the Spirit we can cry out "Abba! Father!" (Gal 4:6).

Finally, this Advocate-Spirit will not be simply another divine person to replace Jesus. In a very real sense, he will be Jesus made present in a new way. In a rather daring statement, Raymond Brown has written: "Since the Paraclete can come only when Jesus departs, the Paraclete is the presence of Jesus when Jesus is absent. Jesus' promises to dwell within his disciples are fulfilled in the Paraclete" (*The Gospel according to John*, vol. 2, 1141). In fact, there is no doubt at all that Jesus is more present to us now in the Spirit than he ever was to his disciples in the flesh. The problem is not one of presence but of recognition.

"He will prove the world wrong" (16:8)

Thus far, John has described the role of the Advocate-Spirit in general terms. He is the Spirit of truth who will explain more fully the message of Jesus and will stand with the disciples to defend them from their enemies. In this final reference to the Spirit, John spells out in terse but clear language the way in which the Spirit will defend the message of Jesus by clarifying the differences between his disciples and the world that opposes them.

Jesus has just told his disciples that it will be to their advantage that he goes away because then he will be able to send the Advocate to them. He continues: "And when he comes, he will prove the world wrong about sin and righteousness and judgment" (16:8). There has been much debate about the exact meaning of the Greek verb which is here translated as "to prove wrong." The more common meaning of this verb is "to convince" or "to convict." Such a meaning would be suitable when talking about sin, but it is less fitting when the object is righteousness or judgment. Raymond Brown (*The Gospel according to John,* vol. 2, 705) has chosen the meaning adopted here and most modern translations have followed suit. The sense would be that the Advocate will "prove the world wrong" in three critical areas of human life, namely, the nature of sin and its opposite, righteousness or justice, and therefore the distinction between them in the process of judgment.

In spite of many centuries of human experience, there is no consensus in our understanding of these three critical factors in human life. Christian believers and secular thinkers are worlds apart in this regard. Hence the necessity of listening to the wisdom of the Spirit. In regard to sin Jesus says that the Spirit will prove the world wrong "about sin, because they do not believe in me" (16:9). The basic meaning of sin is therefore to reject the teaching of Jesus. In particular, this means his teaching that the primary challenge and opportunity of human life is to love unselfishly. Sin means to be egocentric, selfish, controlling, and domineering. To say that this is the way to fulfill one's human destiny and achieve happiness is to live in sinful error.

The counterpart to sin is righteousness or justice or goodness. Jesus says that the Spirit will prove the world wrong "about righteousness, because I am going to the Father and you will see me no longer" (16:10). It is not so easy to see how the departure of Jesus and his return to the Father would expose the nature of righteousness or goodness, as opposed to sinfulness. However, when we see what his return to the Father means, the matter becomes clearer. Those who reject the teaching of Jesus must also reject his claim to be a true prophet—one who comes from God and speaks for God. They think that he is a fraud and that his message will die with him in ignominy. The fact that he returns to his Father in glory is proof positive that he truly came from God and that his teaching is therefore from God and represents the true meaning of righteousness or goodness in our lives. When Jesus says, "you will see me no longer," it is more than simply spelling out the consequence of his departure. It also means that our journey leads us too back to the Father, so that our friends will see us no longer, but that is not so bad because they will see us again if they make the same journey of loving service.

Jesus says finally that the Spirit will prove the world wrong "about judgment, because the ruler of this world has been condemned" (16:11). The ruler or prince of this world is Satan, or the devil, who is the great deceiver. When Jesus dies on the cross it appears that the devil and his allies are right in judging him an impostor who misleads his followers. However, his glorious resurrection and return to his Father proves that the real deceiver is Satan and that it is he and his allies who mislead the people. The resurrection turns everything upside down so that those who thought they had defeated Jesus are suddenly exposed as the ones who are defeated and discredited. It is the role of the Advocate-Spirit to convince the followers of Jesus that the resurrection has indeed happened and that their choice of loving service will be fully vindicated at the end.

All of this can be readily related to the contemporary struggle between secular humanism and religion. The secular contention is that everything happens in the here-and-now and must make sense in terms of this world. The religious conviction is that the here-and-now is only part of a much larger picture, which must also include the divine or transcendent world. For the secularist sin means not to succeed by this world's definition and virtue means to be successful here, even if that means using power and control to achieve one's objectives. From the religious perspective, being successful means to be a loving, caring person who subordinates power and control to loving purposes. The outcome of this radical disagreement in these critical areas will not be known until we reach that other world. Then, if the message of Jesus is true, we will find that God confirms and rewards the simple goodness of those who have made unselfish behavior the primary concern in their lives.

One can observe a similar contrast on the cultural and political level. From the secular perspective, sin means failure to respect the order established and protected by the power brokers of this world. This is called being a "good citizen" or being "patriotic." King Ahab called the prophet Elijah a "troubler of Israel," whereas in reality it was Ahab, wielding royal power, who had corrupted Israel's soul (1 Kgs 18:17ff.). By contrast, for religious persons, sin is failure to love as Jesus loved and it is virtuous to challenge an unjust and oppressive order in society. Such persons are truly good citizens because they strive for reform when that is needed, thus avoiding a blind and uncritical patriotism.

For secular persons, righteousness or goodness is to support the established order even when it is unjust. "Law and order" is their slogan even though the best example of "law and order" in the Bible was the situation in Egypt under the pharaoh. It was law and order for the ruling elite but slavery for the Hebrews. Such a position is said to be "prudent" and "realistic." Moreover, it is said to be validated by material success. By contrast, religious persons find righteousness and goodness in the example of Jesus, which subordinates material success to loving service to those in need. Such persons do not presume to know who is "deserving" but reach out to all without exception. Because this path alone leads to the Father, it alone constitutes real and ultimate human success.

Finally, for those who live by secular wisdom, the death of Jesus in ignominy demonstrates that his way is foolish and misguided. It may be admirable in some ways, but it is credible only to those who live by faith. The resurrection is only an opinion to secular persons and certainly not something to cause them to change their lives. For Christians, by contrast, the resurrection is the most important event in human history because it vindicates the teaching of Jesus as the only ultimately valid wisdom for us humans. It also means that Satan has been found guilty of enticing us to pursue the folly of selfish behavior and thus leading us to tragedy. It is this contrast that the Advocate-Spirit wants to make clear. No issue is more important for us humans.

"He will declare to you the things that are to come" (16:13)

Since the vindication and rewards of a virtuous life will not be fully known in this world, it is essential for the Christian to have a strong sense of hope. Supporting this hope is one of the primary functions of the Advocate-Spirit. The words of Jesus are explicit: "When the Spirit of truth comes, he will guide you into all the truth; for he will not speak on his own, but will speak whatever he hears, and he will declare to you the things that are to come" (16:13). The Spirit will reveal the deeper meaning of the teaching of Jesus and that means that he will tell us what we desperately need to know about the future.

For nonbelievers the future can be very problematic. It is a land of opportunity for those who are young and healthy and talented. As the inevitable aging process sets in, however, the future becomes more and more forbidding. It can only mean further weakness, the need to abandon favorite projects, and finally the specter of sickness and death. Those who have no faith, or whose faith is weak, will generally try simply to avoid thinking about the future. Denial will become a daily exercise. As one is drawn ever more deeply into this threatening prospect, it will be tempting to turn one's back to the future and to try to live off the memories of earlier and more pleasant times.

Those who allow themselves to be guided by the Spirit into the deeper meaning of the teaching of Jesus will come to trust more and more the promises of God that illuminate the future and turn it into a land of hope. St. Paul provides a kind of existential portrayal of this process: "So we do not lose heart. Even though our outer nature is wasting away, our inner nature is being renewed day by day. For this slight momentary affliction is preparing us for an eternal weight of glory beyond all measure . . ." (2 Cor 4:16-17). The Spirit thus nourishes our awareness of God's promises and illuminates the horizon of our lives.

When I was a small boy in boarding school, I recall how differently I experienced the journey by train to and from my home in the mountains of western Pennsylvania. On the way home the scenery was beautiful beyond compare, just as it was drab and forbidding when I had to return to school. If we were as sensitive as we should be to the guidance of the Spirit, our journey into the future would also be filled with joyful expectation—and even more so as we come nearer to our true homeland. That is why the faith witness of an older person is so precious because it demonstrates the victory of hope over despair in a human life precisely when, humanly speaking, there seems to be little reason for hope.

"Your pain will turn into joy" (16:20)

The pain that Jesus is talking about is not just the pain that accompanies his own passion. It is also the pain of all those who follow him, including the Johannine community as it struggles to maintain its morale in the midst of enemies. Once again, we need to be aware of the two levels of meaning in these texts. They are true of Jesus but also of his followers, both at the end of the first century and in our own day. Jesus is very straightforward about this:

> Very truly, I tell you, you will weep and mourn, but the world will rejoice; you will have pain, but your pain will turn into joy. When a woman is in labor, she has pain, because her hour has come. But when her child is born, she no longer remembers the anguish because of the joy of having brought a human being into the world. So you have pain now; but I will see you again, and your hearts will rejoice, and no one will take your joy from you (16:20-22).

Jesus teaches a tough love. It can be very painful to remain faithful to his teaching when everyone is saying that such fidelity is foolishness. Most mothers can verify the analogy used by Jesus. Nine months is a long time and there is often illness and always discomfort. But when the newborn child is seen and is held in one's arms, it all seems a small price to pay for such exquisite joy. These words of Jesus are precious because they are so comforting. As we are buffeted by hopelessness and weakness and pain, the promise of ultimate joy from one who knows all about pain must surely be a great support and consolation. And Jesus tells us also how to pray at such times: "Very truly, I tell you, if you ask anything of the Father in my name, he will give it to you. . . . Ask and you will receive, so that your joy may be complete" (16:23-24).

"I have conquered the world" (16:33)

In the final verses of chapter 16, Jesus promises to speak more clearly about these matters in the future and the disciples claim to understand him now at last. But he is not so sure. "Do you now believe? The hour is coming, indeed it has come, when you will be scattered, each one to his home, and you will leave me alone" (16:31-32). They still have much to learn about their own resources. There is no place here for bravado but only for a humble reliance on divine help. And no one can ask for help with more assurance of a positive response than disciples who are trying to be faithful. Even in his apparent weakness and vulnerability Jesus is very strong because the Father is with him (16:32).

Since his suffering is the suffering of one who loves, it will lead to wonderful victory. The world, with all its apparent power, is no match for those who love. To these Jesus says, "take courage; I have conquered the world" (16:33). He does not conquer through his resurrection but through his loving, which leads to resurrection. When Jesus says that he has conquered the world, it is clear that this reflects a post-resurrection situation. Accordingly, these discourses truly pertain to the world of his disciples, both in the Johannine community and in the ages that follow.

7

That They May Be One

In chapter 17 the situation changes significantly as Jesus directs his words to his heavenly Father rather than to his disciples: "After Jesus had spoken these words, he looked up to heaven and said, 'Father, the hour has come . . .'" (17:1). It is clear, however, that Jesus wants his disciples (and all of us) to hear these words spoken to the Father. And as we eavesdrop on these intimate words we are struck by their sublime content and realize that attempts at interpretation will always be inadequate. What is really called for is personal experience, more than rational probing. In fact, the ideal attitude would be a calm, contemplative gaze rather than an impatient, analytical examination. Only such respectful pondering will enable us to "locate" the mysterious presence of God and thus prepare the way for loving adoration.

"The hour has come" (17:1)

We recall that Jesus spoke about his "hour" already at Cana where he told his mother, "My hour has not yet come" (2:4). And on two other occasions it is said that he could not be taken into custody because his hour had not yet come (7:30

and 8:20). Finally, and surprisingly, when his disciples tell him that some Greeks are asking to see him, he replies, "The hour has come for the Son of Man to be glorified" (12:23). This mysterious "hour" is undoubtedly the time of his passion, death, and resurrection.

We have already noted that the inquiry by the Greeks probably signals the readiness of all humankind to receive the message of Jesus. However, we sense a special urgency to these words in the present context. It is as if the audience has gathered and the curtain is rising. Therefore, when Jesus now tells his Father that his hour has come, it means that all is ready, the stage is set and it is time to begin the final act of this drama.

"Glorify your Son so that the Son may glorify you" (17:1)

When the Bible speaks of the glorification of a person, it means the external manifestation of that person's deeper, hidden nature. Jesus knows that he is playing a role in the drama of salvation scripted by his Father. The ultimate purpose of this role is to make evident in our world the true, hidden nature of God. When Jesus asks his Father to glorify him, therefore, he is asking that the drama be brought to its climax. Jesus has already revealed the glory of God in his miracles of healing and in his hope-filled words, but the full revelation of the love and goodness of God will occur only when Jesus gives his life for us. In other words, Jesus is asking his Father to lead him now to his passion and death.

The glorification of Jesus manifests his love to the whole world. This is not a self-glorification because it is self-giving. And in the very act by which Jesus' true motives are revealed, he glorifies the Father also. The Father is in fact that wonderfully transcendent, but largely unknown, Person who created the world but whose actions are often misunderstood as he is blamed for everything from natural disasters to personal tragedies. Jesus came to make known the true nature of this hidden God, not just by talking about him, but especially by identifying with him. This identification of Jesus with the

Father in his ultimate act of love is reflected in the words of Jesus to Philip: "Whoever has seen me has seen the Father" (14:9).

"And this is eternal life" (17:3)

Eternal life certainly has significant characteristics in common with the mortal life that we all know. However, it is also vastly different from our life precisely because it is impervious to the ravages of disease and death. If we are young and strong and free enough, we may think at times that we have a glimpse of what this kind of life would be like. In fact, however, even these glimpses are really only a momentary sense of being carefree, whereas eternal life is not the absence of care but the fullness of confidence.

John's Gospel is all about the gift of eternal life. At the end of the Gospel, he writes: "Now Jesus did many other signs in the presence of his disciples, which are not written in this book. But these are written so that you may come to believe that Jesus is the Messiah, the Son of God, and that through believing you may have life in his name" (20:30-31). Eternal life is God's own life and, because God loves us, he wants to share it with us. Thus, our wildest dreams can be realized.

In these final dramatic words, addressed to his Father, Jesus sums up the secret of participating in divine life. "And this is eternal life, that they may know you, the only true God, and Jesus Christ whom you have sent" (17:3). It should be obvious that "knowing" the only true God and Jesus, his Son, means much more than having information about them. This kind of knowing is a mystical, intuitive, and experiential union with God; it is entering into that wonderful, personal mystery which good biblical interpretation "locates" for us. Locating it is not, of course, the same as possessing it. That happens only when, through the gift of faith, one surrenders to the wonderful goodness that is at the center of that mystery. Moreover, there is no end to the possibilities of union with that divine center of goodness. For one can never be finished with "knowing" the only true God, and Jesus Christ whom he has sent.

"Father, glorify me in your own presence" (17:5)

Jesus tells his Father that he has already glorified him and revealed his goodness by finishing the work that was assigned to him (17:4). He has already been a loving presence to us all by his miracles and good words. But now it is time to continue and fulfill that work and Jesus describes this climactic moment as his own glorification in the presence of the Father. For what happens on earth is only a pale reflection of the real drama that occurs in heaven. The great public events on earth may have little significance in heaven where value is determined by love rather than power.

The glorification that Jesus seeks in the presence of his Father is said to be "the glory that I had in your presence before the world existed" (17:5). Jesus is praying for the restoration of the glory that he enjoyed as the eternal Word prior to creation and prior to his mission in our human history. But I think there is more implied than that. Later, we hear Jesus saying: "Father, I desire that those also, whom you have given me, may be with me where I am, to see my glory, which you have given me because you loved me before the foundation of the world" (17:24). Jesus does not want to return to his previous glory and leave us behind. He has acquired friends during his mission on earth and he wants them (and all of us) to return with him to the presence of his Father. We can scarcely imagine how delightful it will be to make this journey with him.

"They have believed that you sent me" (17:8)

Jesus reflects on his earthly mission and sums it up by saying to his Father, "I have made your name known to those whom you gave me from the world" (17:6). In a world of shadows and illusions, Jesus has told us that the center and measure of reality is the God who told Moses that his name is "I am" (Exod 3:14). This God is the ultimate reality, and all other reality is to be evaluated in relation to him and to his will. This is so, first of all, because he alone is the creator of all things. More than that, he has shown his love by creating a chosen people from the nothingness of slavery and, in these last days, by sending his only Son to give his life for the liberation of all human beings.

Jesus reminds his Father also that some at least of those whom the Father entrusted to his care have listened to his words and trusted them. They have believed that Jesus does indeed speak for God and that his wisdom deserves to be embraced. This has not been easy for them because unselfish loving is very difficult, and the alternatives are very attractive. Nonetheless, they have trusted the words that the Father gave him and "they have received them and know in truth that I came from you; and they have believed that you sent me" (17:8). It may be worth mentioning again that these words of Jesus are not about rituals and doctrines, important as those things are, but they represent a call to total self-giving in loving devotion to others. This is the message that comes from the Father, and is therefore both incredibly challenging and utterly trustworthy.

"I have been glorified in them" (17:10)

Jesus now extends his concern to those beyond the disciples. When he considers this larger arena, he must declare his attitude toward the world. What he says seems to be incompatible with his usual loving concern: "I am not asking on behalf of the world, but on behalf of those whom you gave me" (17:9). This does not mean that Jesus is excluding most people from his prayerful concern, for all people, without exception, have been entrusted to him by his Father. But he cannot pray for their success as long as they remain part of the hostile world. Rather, he prays that the world, understood as a good creation gone bad, should simply cease to exist. In that sense, one can say that he does not pray for them as a hostile world, but he prays instead for their conversion from that sad condition.

The world beyond the disciples may indeed represent opposition to Jesus, but he is well aware that it is the Father's intention that all creation should belong to him. When he says, "All mine are yours, and yours are mine; and I have been glorified in them" (17:10), he is referring to all of creation, including inanimate beings. (In the Greek, "all" here is neuter plural, more accurately translated as "all things.") Jesus is glorified, i.e., recognized as one who loves, in all of creation, on condition that we know how to read its message. Not only good people reflect the goodness of Jesus; his beauty and kindness are reflected in every flower and in every gentle breeze. If our eyes are open and our ears properly attuned, everything speaks to us of Jesus and celebrates his goodness. At least, this is the way that God has planned it to be.

"Holy Father, protect them in your name" (17:11)

When Jesus calls his heavenly Father "holy," he is using the term in a biblical sense and not as we commonly understand it. When we speak of "holiness," we usually mean moral rectitude or sanctity. In the Bible, however, this word refers more commonly to a state of consecration or of being set apart for religious purposes. We often use the word "sacred" to convey this idea, as in "the sacred vessels of the altar." Jesus' Father is called holy, therefore, because he is wonderfully transcendent, set apart from all that is imperfect and impermanent. As such, he possesses a power that is greater than any power that we know and also unique because it is totally in service of his love.

Jesus asks his Father to use his power to protect all those who have taken the risk of following him. When he says, "protect them in your name," he is asking that the Father keep them safe by embracing them with his presence. For the name of the Father is "I am" (Exod 3:14), which really means, "I am with you." Hence, the Father is asked to remember his covenant commitment and to throw the mantle of his loving care over those who have entered that covenant of love. Jesus says then that this name has been given to him because he is the extension of the Father's love into the world in a way that had never before been seen.

"So that they may be one" (17:11)

The intended result of this protective love will be "so that they may be one, as we are one" (17:11). This prayer for unity will become ever more urgent as Jesus continues to speak to his Father. Since this is so important to him it should also be a primary concern for us. The greatest danger here is that we may confuse "unity" with "uniformity," which is a superficial kind of unity that is concerned only with appearances. Thus, a group of people may dress alike, and therefore look alike, but still be far from united in their hearts. However, since true internal unity is so difficult to achieve, we are often tempted to settle for some kind of uniformity.

The radical difference between unity and uniformity becomes evident when we note that true unity allows for and even encourages a real *lack* of uniformity. For true unity is the result of our love for one another, and such love desires that we all be our true and unique selves. St. Paul makes all this very clear in his discussion of the dynamics of a successful Christian community in 1 Corinthians 12. Adopting the analogy of a human body, he points out how important it is that each member of the body be affirmed and thanked for its unique role. But this can be achieved in the Christian community only if destructive competition is abandoned and is replaced by loving concern for others. And then he writes about the qualities of that unselfish love in the famous 1 Corinthians 13. It is this kind of unity, resulting from mutual love and encouraging diversity, that Jesus asks for in this final, earnest prayer.

This prayer of Jesus for unity has rightly been recognized as the ideal basis for a continuing and urgent search for unity among all those who believe in God. This does not mean that some must "win," while others "lose," because all religious traditions have beautiful and valid elements that deserve to be honored and preserved. Diversity will, in fact, be the hallmark of a unified community of believers. But there will also need to be a genuine love and trust among all the members, and that will necessarily involve genuine forgiveness for past failings. Moreover, if we read carefully these words of Jesus, we cannot conclude that this is just another optional issue to be considered when we have time for it, which probably means never.

Surely one of the first questions asked of us at the final judgment will be, "What have you done to heal the wounds of division among you?"

"That they may have my joy" (17:13)

Jesus has prayed that all his followers may be united in mutual love and trust. In a sense, that is the first fruit of his final prayer. His second desire is that they may all participate in his joy. Joy is a kind of exuberant awareness that all is well; it bubbles up from a deep sense of confidence and peace. Jesus knows that he is united with his heavenly Father and that all fear and anxiety will pass away and leave only the joy of being in touch with the source of life and happiness. This kind of joy, since it comes from a deep mystical union with God, can survive even the most severe storms of life.

Jesus not only prays that we may participate in his joy but "that they may have my joy made complete in themselves" (17:13). This clearly implies that there are degrees of participation in his joy and that it is only through patience and perseverance that the fullness of his joy can be ours. Contrary to the morose and pessimistic predictions of our secular culture, this joy can increase even as we grow older. It is worth citing again the comforting words of St. Paul: "So we do not lose heart. Even though our outer nature is wasting away, our inner nature is being renewed day by day" (2 Cor 4:16). The renewal of our inner nature is the victory of joy and hope over anxiety and despair. It is consoling to know that this is one of the primary elements in the prayer of Jesus. The only thing that can prevent us from feeling the effect of this powerful prayer is our lack of trust.

"Protect them from the evil one" (17:15)

There is no doubt about the identity of the evil one in John's Gospel; it is Satan or the devil. And John is also careful to let us know why we need to be protected from his influence. We read in 8:44 that "he was a murderer from the beginning and does not stand in the truth, because there is no truth in him. When he lies, he speaks according to his own nature, for he is a liar and the father of lies." Jesus told Pilate that the whole purpose of his becoming one of us is to teach us the truth about the meaning and purpose of our existence. And this truth is that we must allow ourselves to be loved into freedom, and then must use that freedom for loving service, so that others also may be free. Satan is a liar and deceiver because he tells us that this teaching of Jesus is not only difficult but that it is also untrue. The devil suggests that we should seek happiness by forgetting that our freedom is a gift as we use it to dominate others. In fact, if people stand in our way, we must simply use our superior strength to push them aside.

If Satan's interpretation of our purpose in life were obvious nonsense, we could easily dismiss him and he would not be a threat to us. From a merely human or rational point of view, however, what he tells us makes very good sense and seems to be the only way that is really promising. Nonetheless, since God made us good, there is a deep inner awareness that unselfish loving is the good and noble thing to do. That deep instinct is easily suppressed by massive pragmatic evidence to the contrary. It just seems too idealistic, especially when it doesn't pay off in the short term. It is through the gift of faith that we are able to recover that original instinct for good and to trust its effectiveness for ultimate success and happiness.

It is not hard to see, therefore, that we are involved in a dramatic struggle and that the stakes could not be higher. Most of us are tempted to straddle the issue, recognizing the wisdom of Jesus but frequently living in accordance with the devil's suggestion. This issue is so important that we find it highlighted already in the covenant of God with Israel. They experienced the love of God and were empowered by it to leave the place of bondage. But their much greater discovery was the implications of this divine action in their own behavior. God did not choose the Hebrew slaves because they were more attractive than the Egyptians (or any other nation). He chose them because *he is good,* and it is of the nature of goodness to love and assist those who are most in need. Whether we think they deserve it is totally irrelevant; the only thing that matters is that they need help.

When the Israelites experienced this unconditional love of God and acquired freedom and confidence because of it, they had to wonder about what this might mean in regard to their own freedom and ability to love. They had good reason to wonder because this was the center of their new covenant obligation as God's chosen people. All this is clearly portrayed in a beautiful text from Deuteronomy: "You shall not deprive a resident alien or an orphan of justice; you shall not take a widow's garment in pledge. Remember that you were a slave in Egypt and the Lord your God redeemed you from there; *therefore I command you to do this"* (24:17-18, emphasis added).

Thus the Israelites are told that in their dealings with others they must never take advantage of weaker persons, such as the widow or the orphan or the alien, but that they must care for these people and help them to become strong. Why are they expected to do what other nations do not do? Because they alone have seen how God uses his own freedom and henceforth they know *what the purpose of freedom is.* Freedom is not for dominating others and for seizing whatever one wants; its only legitimate purpose is to love others and free them and give them confidence, just as God has done for Israel. To be God's people means to use freedom as God uses freedom, and this alone brings his human creatures to happiness and fulfillment.

When Jesus prays to his heavenly Father, therefore, asking him to protect us from the evil one, he is talking about helping us in this most fundamental of all moral struggles. Are we to use what freedom we have to help others so that they may become more free and perhaps future rivals, or are we to try to better our own position so that we can survive in a highly competitive world? The Christian answer is contained in the truth that Jesus teaches and which takes issue with the big lie of Satan. This truth of Jesus, which sums up his entire mission and ministry, is that we are called to be unselfish. How unselfish? As much as we possibly can be, which is probably a little more than we think is possible! Does this really pay off? Perhaps not immediately, although it will often bring real satisfaction, but decidedly so at the time of judgment.

"Sanctify them in the truth; your word is truth" (17:17)

We come now to a real climax in this final prayer of Jesus. Jesus asks his heavenly Father to sanctify his disciples (and all of us) in the truth, which is identified as the Father's word. This is the very same truth to which Jesus referred in his dialogue with Pilate in the last moments of his life. "For this I was born, and for this I came into the world, to testify to the truth" (18:37). Thus, the whole mission of Jesus among us is somehow connected to the revelation of this supreme truth. As we have already noted, this truth is not some philosophical verity, which we are asked to admire or which may somehow resonate with our intellectual mood. Rather, it is the revelation by the Father, in Jesus Christ, of the whole purpose and meaning of our existence as human beings. Moreover, it is not just what Jesus teaches; it is embodied in the actions and the person of Jesus himself.

In a word, this truth is the unveiling of the reality of God's unconditional love for us. This divine love is incarnate in the person of Jesus who offers it to us every minute of every day. And it is the gift of faith that enables us to trust this revelation, in spite of frequently massive evidence to the contrary. For faith enables us to see that, beneath the surface flow of much sin and violence, there is a deep river of goodness which we are invited to tap and make available to others. To be sanctified in the truth is to be fully committed to this radical interpretation of life, even though it may seem foolish at times, for in the end it will prove to be the only wisdom.

When Jesus asks his Father to sanctify us in the truth, he is praying that we may become one with himself in belonging totally to the Father. This means that we are called to live in the presence and warmth of the Father's incredible love and to trust the hidden goodness in life, just as Jesus lives in the Father's bosom and listens to his heartbeat. And this is just another way of saying what has already been noted when Jesus asks the Father to "protect them in your name" (17:11). This is not, therefore, a question of moral holiness but of something much deeper which makes moral uprightness possible. Jesus wants nothing less than that we enjoy, in the measure possible to mere mortals, the same vital relationship with the Father which is his own prerogative as divine Son.

In a certain sense, Jesus wants us to look beyond himself to the One whose loving goodness gave us life in the first place and whose loving goodness enables us to make the most of that gift of life. People who seek holiness for its own sake are in grave danger of pursuing a selfish enterprise. Jesus prays that we may discover the goodness of his Father and then, in the freedom and confidence that comes from that discovery, that we choose to be a loving gift in the lives of others. When that happens, holiness will follow of its own accord and, at the same time, the ever-present danger of pride will be eliminated.

"And for their sakes I sanctify myself, so that they also may be sanctified in truth" (17:19)

When Jesus says that he sanctifies himself for our sakes, he is referring to his total self-giving, which reached its climax in his sacrificial death on the cross. Ignace de la Potterie points out that this sacrifice must not be limited to the dying of Jesus but comprehends his whole life of obedience to the Father's plan for him (*La Vérité dans Saint Jean,* 761). Moreover, this obedience is not just accepting the will of another; it comes from an awareness of love that produces total trust. The union of Jesus with his Father is so intimate that the Father's will is simply part and parcel of his overwhelming love.

For this reason it could never have been sufficient for Jesus simply to tell us about the love of God; he felt compelled to live it, and thus to make it incarnate in our world. Since this love is expressed primarily in his dying, it is clear that it is not a romantic infatuation but the authentic, unselfish loving that always involves dying for the sake of another. This is that "foolish" loving that turns out to be the only wisdom.

The unselfish purpose for which Jesus offers himself is that we also may be "sanctified in truth" (17:19). The phrase, "in truth," can mean simply "in reality." However, it is almost certain that it refers to the truth of revelation that Jesus offers to us. It would mean then that we fulfill the hopes of Jesus when we follow his lead and live in the liberating love of the Father which in turn enables us, indeed impels us, to join Jesus in his dying for others.

All this is reflected in the format of the Eucharist where we hear, first of all, in the readings, about the goodness and mercy of God—in creation, in the story of Israel and in the loving ministry of Jesus himself. The Eucharistic Prayer then takes us into the mystery of the re-enactment of the dying and rising of Jesus as the fullness of his love is revealed. And by receiving his Body and Blood in Holy Communion we joyfully commit ourselves to make his love present in every aspect of our lives as we return to our homes and our work. All of this is possible only to the extent that we can, like Jesus, live in the love of the Father. This divine love is the sunshine toward which we turn our hungry petals to be energized for loving service to others.

"So that the world may believe that you have sent me" (17:21)

Jesus now looks beyond his disciples to those who have not yet known him. The Father's love embraces all of creation and the love of Jesus is just as limitless. But he knows that he is leaving us and, though he will continue to be present in the Spirit, he wants us to know that our cooperation will be indispensable in fulfilling his loving purposes. Once again, this cooperation demands much more than merely telling others about the love of Jesus for them. That message must be part of the very lives of those who bear witness. The words of Jesus are explicit: "As you, Father, are in me and I am in you, *may they also be in us,* so that the world may believe that you have sent me" (17:21, emphasis added). To be in Jesus and in the Father means to be filled with the flow of love that courses between them and into which all of us are invited.

One senses a real urgency in these words of Jesus. He knows how wonderful it is to be transformed by the love of God and, since this love must reach out to others, he is impatient to share it with all of us. He knows full well that those who are afraid of the sacrifice implied in this kind of loving may draw back and continue to live outside the circle of his love. Moreover, if they persist in this tragic choice, they will eventually fall out of his orbit altogether and be lost in the cold and darkness of outer space.

In the early centuries of the Church, the doxology at the end of liturgical prayers was much more expressive as it suggested the roles of each of the divine Persons of the Trinity: "Glory be to the Father, through the Son, in the Holy Spirit." We praise the Father as the source of all goodness, and we recognize that this goodness comes to us through the loving sacrifice of the Son, and we realize that our incorporation into this flow of love is the work of the Spirit, who helps us to return our praise and service to the Father through the Son. In this earnest prayer, Jesus asks that we who have felt his love may gladly accept our responsibility to bring others into the flow of love that constitutes the heart of the Trinity.

"Righteous Father, the world does not know you" (17:25)

Those who have not yet been warmed by the love of the Father may very well have some concept of God, but what they see is only the all-powerful creator. And when they note how much violence there is in his creation, they are more than ready to reject such a God as unworthy of their respect and homage. Jesus does not deny the power of God and he knows that power alone can be very cruel. But his whole mission is focused

on the revelation of the love of God. Nor is this love an at-
tribute that merely co-exists with God's power. In fact, his
power is totally in the service of his love. It is this important
fact that is not generally known and it is to the revelation of
this primacy of God's love that Jesus devotes his life.

When Jesus calls his Father "righteous," he uses the term
in a biblical sense, which emphasizes the goodness and mercy
of God. We note the same meaning in the infancy story of
Matthew's Gospel where it is said that Joseph did not wish to
expose Mary to public disgrace because he was "a righteous
man" (1:19). What is at issue is not equity but loving sensitivity. When we read in John's Prologue that "no one has ever
seen God" (1:18), we recognize a parallel statement to "the
world does not know you" (17:25). And just as Jesus continues
here with the words "but I know you," so also we read in the
Prologue, "It is God the only Son, who is close to the Father's
heart, who has made him known" (1:18). Jesus knows God as
loving Father and not just as powerful creator; he has listened
to his heartbeat; he knows his goodness and wants all of us to
know it too. And when we do, we will never live in fear again.

Jesus ends this final discourse with the words: "I made
your name known to them, and I will make it known, so that
the love with which you have loved me may be in them, and I
in them" (17:26). In his public ministry Jesus reflected the love
and concern which reveal the true nature of God. But it is primarily in his passion and death that he makes that love so evident that no one has any right to question it again. For he gives
his very life so that we may experience the liberating love of
the Father and, to the extent that this happens, we are liberated from every bond of guilt and fear. At that point, Jesus can
say, "I am in them" (17:26).

It is important to imitate Jesus but sometimes we forget
that the best way to do this is simply to accept God as Jesus
did, that is, as wonderfully loving parent. More than anything
else, Jesus wants us to imitate him in that way and, to the extent that we are able to do so, we become one with him and we

begin to understand the truth which is his best gift to us. To be in touch with this truth is to live in mystical union with the Father, in Jesus, and through the transforming presence of the Holy Spirit.

8

Conversion

We have seen how the members of the Johannine community are deepening their appreciation of the death and resurrection of Jesus with the aid of the Advocate/Spirit. But they are also participating in the sacraments of the Church. These include in particular the two major sacraments of initiation, i.e., baptism and Eucharist, which presuppose, of course, an original conversion. Under the pressure of persecution, it has become increasingly clear to them that the most important element in these sacraments is not the external ritual, which in their situation may have been curtailed, but the living faith of the participants.

All of this helps to explain the organization of the first half of John's Gospel. Though it appears to be simply stories from Jesus' public ministry, it is in fact a revisiting of the stages of Christian initiation and growth under the guise of the experience of Jesus in the days before his death and resurrection. This is the contention of L. William Countryman, who has suggested that all of the public ministry stories in John's Gospel are to be understood on two levels, namely, that of the experience of Jesus himself and then of the experience of Christians in their sacramental and mystical growth into an ever more perfect union with Christ. Countryman writes that

> the Gospel of John is structured according to the experience of the believer. . . . Writing for a Christian audience, John presents the mystical path as the continuation of their existing religious experience. Conversion, baptism, and reception of the Eucharist lead on without a break (though not by any sort of inevitability) to mystical enlightenment and union (*The Mystical Way in the Fourth Gospel*, 2nd ed., 1–2).

Countryman argues, therefore, that the first half of John's Gospel (after the Prologue) not only deals occasionally with the stages of Christian growth but is actually organized according to those stages. Thus, conversion is the subject of the entire section from 1:19 to 2:25, including the Cana miracle and the cleansing of the temple, since they also deal with change or conversion. (Countryman begins this section at 1:35, but I prefer to retain the traditional structure.) Baptism, which logically follows conversion, is the subject of the entire section from 3:1 to 5:47 because water is involved also in the story of the woman at the well and the cripple at the pool of Bethesda. Eucharist would be the subject of 6:1 to 7:52, which is about the bread of life and the water that quenches thirst.

At this point, John invites Christians to deepen their union with Christ through mystical enlightenment (8:12 to 9:41), signaled by Jesus' claim to be the "light of the world" and illustrated by the story of the blind man. Finally, the disciples are invited to discover the fullness of life under the protection of the Good Shepherd and with Lazarus who is raised from the dead (10:1 to 11:44).

This is therefore the final step in the thematic approach that we have chosen. Although this procedure seems to be reversing the flow of the gospel narrative, it is in fact following the actual process by which the community of John grew toward a deep mystical awareness of their union with Christ. We recall that the first step was the discovery that Jesus was not defeated but that in him God had conquered death and given hope to all mortal human beings. The truly revolutionary element in this discovery was the awareness that this victory came through the loving self-offering of Jesus. They recognized then that the central revelation that Jesus brought—the ultimate truth—was that unselfish loving is the only way for human beings to conquer death with Jesus.

At a second stage these first Christians deepened their understanding of how the love of Jesus could become part of their own loving in all the many areas of their human lives. This deeper understanding came about through the subtle but powerful influence of the Advocate-Spirit who was sent to them by the risen Lord. All the implications of this work of the Spirit are the subject of the farewell discourses of Jesus where he is pictured telling them, before his death, what that death through love would mean in their day-to-day lives.

At a third stage, in the fifty plus years that separated the death of Jesus from the composition of this Gospel, they have been discovering the meaning of Jesus in their lives through the more formal and ecclesiastical medium of the Christian sacraments. They have also discovered that the sacraments are not an end in themselves but a means that can lead them safely to a personal, mystical union with God in Christ. It is this mystical experience of God that they see to be the fulfillment of their destiny and the sure path to eternal life. It is not surprising then that they should have interwoven, as it were, the public ministry of Jesus and their own sacramental journey toward true life.

"Who are you?" (1:19)

The subject of conversion is introduced by a reference to the role of John the Baptist who signals a break from the rigid structures of religion represented by the temple establishment. Priests and Levites are sent from Jerusalem to the Jordan River, where John has been baptizing. They are on a mission of inquiry. He is performing a religious ritual and it is obvious that he has not consulted them beforehand. They want to know who he claims to be. Is he the Messiah? The answer is "No." Is he Elijah, expected to precede the Messiah, or perhaps the prophet promised by Moses for the last days (Deut 18:15)? The answer again is "No." One has the distinct impression that John the Baptist is fully prepared to say "No" to every question they propose, for he has come to announce radical change and they are dedicated to the status quo. They represent the established order, which wishes to preserve itself at all cost; he represents the new divine order, which will challenge all human arrangements that are not open to God's sovereignty in matters of salvation.

When John the Baptist does finally speak in a positive manner, he identifies himself as the one whom Isaiah had in mind when he wrote, "I am the voice of one crying out in the wilderness, 'Make straight the way of the Lord'" (Isa 40:3; John 1:23). One must wonder what the emissaries from Jerusalem may have thought about this answer. They certainly could not have been comforted because the words mean that the coming of the Lord will require that all human obstacles must be removed—a prospect that should strike fear in the hearts of all who want to change nothing. A little later John will characterize his baptism as a provisional rite in preparation for the one who will baptize, not only with water as he has done but now in the creative, radical Spirit of the new age.

"This is the Son of God" (1:34)

The community of John was precocious in its discovery of the full implications of the divinity of Jesus. We are so accustomed to thinking of Jesus in terms of divinity that we forget how difficult it must have been for his Jewish disciples, grounded as they were in the strict monotheism of the Hebrew Scriptures, to come to an understanding of more than one divine person. After the resurrection, they certainly realized that Jesus was far more than the extraordinary human being whom they had come to know. But it would take years for them to move

beyond the stage of wonder to the possibility of a clear declaration of his divinity. And we know that it took the Church
several centuries to find appropriate theological terminology
for this astounding fact. That is why it is so surprising to find
here such explicit and frequent references to the divinity of
Jesus. The best explanation is that the author of John's Gospel
not only had more time to reflect on the implications of the
resurrection (since this Gospel was not written until the 90s)
but that he was also a great mystic and therefore attuned to the
full implications of Jesus' resurrection.

Mysticism has often been misunderstood. It is frequently
associated with extraordinary phenomena, and it is thought to
be the province of a few cloistered monks or nuns who live a
far different life from the one that we are familiar with. It is
also frequently thought to be rather dangerous because it seems
to isolate the mystic from the community and its sacramental
life. The truth is, of course, something quite different. In sim-
plest terms, mystics are those who enjoy a direct and unmediated experience of God. They are able to understand the true
nature and purpose of the many aids or means that seek to put
us in touch with God and to come therefore to a deeply personal and immediate experience of the divinity. The entire created world becomes in a sense transparent as they realize that
God's presence is more real than anything else in creation.

Evelyn Underhill has written extensively on this subject
and she sums it up by saying, "Mysticism is the art of union
with Reality" (*Practical Mysticism*, 3). Even for mystics, however, this consciousness is not a permanent state but usually involves mere glimpses of the transcendent world. Of course,
these glimpses are enough to transform one's evaluation of this
world and of what it offers. Instead of being the only place
where one can find success and happiness, the world becomes
little more than a pale reflection of the real world. Underhill
comments with sadness on the situation where most of us find
ourselves: "Because Mystery is so horrible to us, we have agreed
for the most part to live in a world of labels" (Ibid., 7).

The Beloved Disciple, who shaped the Fourth Gospel, led his community along the mystical path which enabled them to appreciate the divinity of Jesus much sooner than others. This awareness also put them into immediate and dangerous conflict with their Jewish friends and neighbors who thought that they were committing blasphemy when they seemed to be claiming that there was another God other than YHWH, the God of the Hebrew tradition. It is impossible to understand John's Gospel without being aware of the profound influence of the experience of his community on the way the story of Jesus is told. For example, the animosity shown toward the Jews in this Gospel has far more to do with the experience of the Johannine community in the 80s and 90s than it does with the life of Jesus in the late 20s.

"Come and see" (1:39)

The calling of the disciples in John's Gospel obviously pertains to the subject of conversion because they are leaving their former state in order to follow Jesus. John does not follow the Synoptic Gospels in giving us a list of all twelve apostles. Rather, he chooses several disciples who are presented as representatives of certain qualities that must be found in any disciple, including ourselves.

The first example of this is found in the deceptively simple story found in 1:35-39. John the Baptist has just pointed out Jesus with the words, "Look, here is the Lamb of God" (1:36). Two of the Baptist's disciples, upon hearing this, leave him and begin to follow Jesus: "When Jesus turned and saw them following, he said to them, 'What are you looking for?'" (1:38). This apparently casual question, suggesting curiosity, takes on profound significance when we realize that Jesus is, in fact, asking them whether they are, like most human beings, seeking to know the meaning and purpose of life. (It is perhaps not too farfetched to paraphrase the question of Jesus in modern terminology as: Are you earthlings, since I see that you are forever searching for something? After all, in John's Gospel, Jesus would surely be the ultimate E.T. [Extraterrestrial One], for he came from eternity to tell us about the meaning of life on earth!)

Their reply is also a question: "Rabbi (which translated means "Teacher"), where are you staying?" (1:38). On the historical level, there is no reason for them to think that this stranger is a rabbi. However, on the symbolic level, it would be appropriate because they know that anyone who can see so clearly what is in their hearts must indeed be one who has answers to deep questions, that is, a teacher. And when they ask, "Where are you staying?" it would be naive to think that this is simply a question about his place of residence. Furthermore, we are invited to understand this on a symbolic level by the fact, not readily noticed by those who read this only in translation, that the verb for "staying" is the same one used by John to express that profound personal union that exists between himself and his heavenly Father. In such cases it is usually translated as "abide" (see, e.g., 15:4). Suddenly, this question becomes a plea for help in knowing where we questioning human beings can find the peace and happiness that we seek. In fact, I like to think that it would not be farfetched to phrase the question, "Rabbi, where is our true home?"

The answer of Jesus to this most important of all human questions is not, as we might expect, a catechism reference to heaven, but an answer that reveals the primary concern of John's Gospel, namely, the preference of religious experience over conceptual knowledge. And so Jesus replies simply, "Come and see" (1:39). In other words, he invites them (and us) to come to him and to walk with him and to learn from him, for only in this way will we discover the truth about God's love for us, revealed in Jesus, and about our need to join him in loving others. Nothing we can ever learn is more important than this.

It would appear that the words that follow contradict this symbolic interpretation, but there are clear hints that such is not the case. "They came and saw where he was staying, and they remained with him that day. It was about four o'clock in the afternoon" (1:39). First, a "day" in the Bible can mean, not

only a period of twenty-four hours, but also any span of time
that constitutes a special opportunity (cf. e.g., Heb 3:13-14).
But the surprising statement that it was "about four o'clock in
the afternoon" is far more significant since it may very well be
an echo of that fateful question concerning life and death spoken by God to Adam at that very same time in the Garden of
Eden (Gen 3:9)! This interpretation becomes even more plausible when we note that John begins his Gospel with the same
words that open the book of Genesis, a fact that alerts us to al-
lusions to the creation story.

Qualities of Discipleship

From this simple but deeply meaningful episode, we learn
that the first and most important precondition for conversion
is a *profound yearning* for a meaning in life that is more than
what worldly wisdom can offer. Sometimes it takes the shock
of an unexpected accident or illness, or the loss of a family
member or a dear friend, to make us realize that there must be
more to life than we have been led to believe. Accordingly, a
feeling of smug security, which many would consider desirable,
is in fact a symptom of dangerous illness in the realm of spiritual realities.

In 1:40-51 John describes the call of several other disciples, each of whom models a further characteristic of authentic discipleship. The first is Andrew's brother Simon, to
whom Jesus gives the new name of Cephas (in Aramaic) or
Peter (in Greek). It is worth noting that no one was called either Cephas or Peter in those days and therefore the new name
signifies, not a mere identification, but a quality of Peter that
Jesus discerns and approves. Since both of these words mean
"rock," the characteristic represented by Peter is *stability*. To be
a good disciple one must be able to make a firm commitment
and to stay with it through thick and thin. This implies a good
sense of personal identity, which is possible only when one has
experienced the love of God, usually expressed through the
love of good human persons.

Philip then finds Nathaniel and tells him that he has found one who seems to be the promised Messiah, namely, "Jesus son of Joseph from Nazareth" (1:45). Nathaniel is skeptical when he hears that Jesus comes from Nazareth, a small town in Galilee. He asks Philip, "Can anything good come out of Nazareth?" (1:46). Philip suggests that he should trust his intuition rather than human estimation: "Come and see" (1:46). When Jesus sees Nathaniel coming toward him, he says, "Here is truly an Israelite in whom there is no deceit!" (1:47).

Nathaniel understands then that his personal experience is far more trustworthy than his provincial prejudice and exclaims, "Rabbi, you are the Son of God! You are the King of Israel!" (1:49). This rather lengthy exchange indicates the importance that John assigns to the quality of *trusting one's intuition* or *being open to surprise*. Jesus confirms the importance of this attitude with an extraordinary promise: "You will see greater things than these . . . you will see heaven opened and the angels of God ascending and descending upon the Son of Man" (1:50-51). Those who are willing to be led by their personal experience of God will be brought to the mystical heights and there join Jacob who saw the heavens opened and became Israel, the father of God's people (see Gen 28:12).

"You have kept the good wine until now" (2:10)

The miracle of the changing of water into wine at the wedding feast in Cana belongs to the theme of conversion because it signals the kind of radical change that the coming of Jesus represents. In keeping with this imagery, the human experience of life prior to his coming is as bland and colorless as water—not bad, but not festive either. After his coming, however, those who believe in him will see that the world takes on a whole new complexion. It is tasteful and effervescent and exciting. John tells us, therefore, that Jesus has come to change the whole world for those who are ready to trust his message.

The exchange between Jesus and his mother is a secondary theme in this story. This dialogue must be seen in connection with the other place in John's Gospel where Mary is call "woman" by Jesus, namely, at the foot of the cross (19:26-27). This is not the way a son normally speaks to his mother, unless one wishes to give the word special symbolic meaning. Such is clearly the case in this instance where Mary is recognized as the new Eve and will symbolize the Church, mother of all who believe in Jesus. At the Cana miracle, Jesus seems to dismiss her request by saying that his hour has not yet come. He does so because Mary is appealing to him on the basis of her human relationship. When she stands under the cross and thus suffers with him in his "hour," she rises above that human relationship and takes on the role of Mother Church. This is true, first, because she has given birth to Jesus into whom the members of the Church are born through baptism, and also because she will show motherly concern for all those who have become one with her son, Jesus.

"Stop making my Father's house a marketplace" (2:16)

If ever there were an example of change or conversion, it would be the cleansing of the temple by Jesus. We know that this action is placed by the Synoptics at the end of the public ministry of Jesus where it is better situated. It seems rather obvious that John has moved it to the beginning of Jesus' ministry because it belongs to this initial theme of conversion. It is important to realize that Jesus is not driving out the animals and money-changers from the temple area in order to correct some liturgical abuse. His action is symbolic and goes much deeper than a change of temple arrangements. John makes this clear when he says that the disciples, upon seeing what Jesus was doing, remembered the text from the psalms, "Zeal for your house will consume me" (Ps 69:9; John 2:17). This indicates that his action is prophetic and represents a challenge to what the temple has come to signify for the people of that time.

We recall that the emissaries from Jerusalem who questioned the actions of John the Baptist (1:19-27) represented a temple that had become so subject to human control that it was not ready for the coming of the Lord. This is what Jesus finds also. One could easily imagine that Jesus used that whip of cords to take swipes even at the pillars of the temple, for it had become symbolic of a religion that had become so rigid and stagnant that it was unable to welcome the God of change and progress.

We know, of course, that we humans are constantly tempted to forget that, while we must make plans and maintain some kind of order in life, we must also be aware that the creative power of the Spirit may at any moment call for changes that we would tend to resist. There are many signs that John's community saw this happening in other Christian groups who were too tradition-bound to accept their own radical understanding of the divinity of Jesus and their own experience of mystical union with God in Jesus. Of course, not all invitations to change are good—in fact, many are probably bad—but we can be sure that the Spirit is always urging us to change and grow toward an ever more authentic representation of God's love in our world. Accordingly, opposing every change is just as bad as wanting to change everything.

At the end of this section, Jesus makes a mysterious statement about his unwillingness to "entrust himself to them" (2:24). Countryman is surely right in suggesting that this represents a warning about failing to go beyond a merely superficial conversion (*The Mystical Way in the Fourth Gospel*, 2nd ed., 31). Sometimes we may think that, since we were born into the true Church, there is no further need for conversion. Nothing could be farther from the truth. In fact, conversion is the work of a lifetime, for one must constantly examine and improve the quality of one's faith and the depth of one's commitment to the Gospel. We will see that this is true, not only of conversion but of all the stages of our growth into Christ. We must continue to deepen our experience of these stages or risk losing what we have already gained.

9

Baptism

After conversion, the next stage in the believer's initiation into the mystery of Christ is baptism. For John this is not just a ritual event, occurring most likely in our distant infancy, but a continuing personal immersion in our experience of the meaning of the truth, which Jesus came to reveal and to exemplify. This truth, we recall, is the reality of God's love for us and the need for us to respond by living as unselfishly as possible. John is well aware, of course, that there is a ritual involved, and he certainly does not belittle its importance, but he is insistent that we must not be satisfied with this external action which remains essentially inoperative without a free and personal faith commitment.

John deals explicitly with baptism in chapter 3. However, according to L. William Countryman, chapters 4 and 5 also pertain to the theme of baptism because they are concerned with water imagery, as we see in the cases of the woman at the well and the cripple at the pool of Bethesda (*The Mystical Way in the Fourth Gospel*, 2nd ed., 8). Countryman's ingenious suggestion reminds us that the gospel writers were usually far more interested in theology than in history. For it is the experience of the Christian convert that governs the sequence of events in John's Gospel rather than the historical experience of Jesus himself. Thus, what Jesus says to Nicodemus in chapter 3 is intended primarily to explain the meaning of baptism for Christians at the end of the first century. New light is cast on the stories of the woman at the well (chapter 4) and the cripple at the pool of Bethesda (chapter 5), where water imagery connects these stories also to the theme of the meaning of baptism. This suggestion seems to be confirmed by the fact that John places his discussion of the Eucharist in chapter 6, where it follows the treatment of baptism, just as it has always followed baptism in the sacramental experience of Christians.

"No one can see the kingdom of God without being born from above" (3:3)

Nicodemus is identified as a "leader of the Jews" (3:1) and this means that he should be more alert than most to the coming of the Messiah. He comes to Jesus "by night" (3:2), which could mean historically that he did not want his fellow Jews to know about his interest in Jesus but, on a symbolic level, it means that he is leaving the darkness to seek the light of Jesus. He has been impressed by the miracles of Jesus and realizes that he is a man of God. And Jesus wastes no time in delivering a challenging message from God: "Very truly, I tell you, no one can see the kingdom of God without being born from above" (3:3).

Nicodemus may very well have been expecting Jesus to tell him about some new rite to perform or prayer to recite. Instead, he announces the absolute necessity of a new birth. Otherwise, the kingdom, which represents the glories of the messianic age, cannot be attained. The primary characteristic of this new birth or beginning is that it is "from above" (3:3). This phrase translates a Greek adverb that can mean either "from above" or "again." Most translators choose one meaning for the text and place the other in a footnote. However, it is quite possible that the author, being fully aware of the ambiguity, simply intended both meanings. In fact, the birth that

Jesus has in mind is both a new birth and one that is from above, i.e., spiritual. In other words, Jesus has come to initiate a new era in human history and those who wish to be part of it will need to change their lives in a radical way. This will not mean a new diet or a new exercise regimen but a change in basic spiritual values and priorities.

"No one can enter the kingdom of God without being born of water and Spirit" (3:5)

Nicodemus can see only the physical meaning of rebirth and so he is given the role of one who asks a naive question in order to provoke further explanation: "Can one enter a second time into the mother's womb and be born?" (3:4). Jesus immediately expands on his previous statement. He makes it clear, first, that the baptismal ritual is important. To be "born of water" means to go through the rite of baptism. However, this is no longer the ritual of John the Baptist, which was with water only. The new baptism will happen in the Spirit. This kind of birth will be as mysterious as the action of the wind, which, though powerful and sometimes destructive, is nonetheless invisible. It is helpful to note that a single Greek word is used for both "wind" and "spirit."

Throughout the Bible, the Spirit is associated with creation. We recall that the author of Genesis describes the process of original creation as the blowing of a wind/spirit across the watery deep (1:2). This is, in a sense, the breath of God that calls being out of nothingness and "blows" life into the first human being (Gen 2:7). To be "born of the Spirit," therefore, means to discover and to embrace the meaning of life intended by God. It is to choose to accept the gift that enables us to be what God has always wanted us to be, namely, loving, caring human beings. In the Gospel of John, this means to embrace that liberating truth that Jesus came to reveal and to which his whole life was devoted.

When Nicodemus wonders how all this can be (3:9), Jesus reminds him that this kind of wisdom is not acquired by human study but comes only as a gift from God. No doubt John has the Jewish opponents of his community in mind when he shows Jesus wondering how a "teacher of Israel" (3:10) could fail to understand what he has said. But this should not be surprising, either then or today, since this is a wisdom that comes down from heaven and only the Son of Man, who is in touch with both heaven and earth (3:13), can reveal it. He alone has been "close to the Father's heart" (1:18) and knows about God's unconditional love for us. He knows too that this unselfish love must become the ideal in the lives of all of us, as the following passage makes abundantly clear.

"God so loved the world that he gave his only Son" (3:16)

The truth that Jesus came to reveal to us is not concerned with our sinfulness or the inevitability of death or any other discouraging reality. We can discover all those things on our own. He came to reveal to us something that we have great difficulty in believing, that is, that God loves us so much that, if we really understood it, we would not fear anything that could possibly happen to us. Of course, it is easy to say that God is good and loving and merciful. But saying it and knowing it in the depths of one's being are quite different matters. And if there is one thing that is of overriding importance in John's Gospel, it is the desire to lead us from a merely verbal and superficial form of faith to a deeply personal experience of the love of God.

The text of 3:16 continues, "so that everyone who believes in him may not perish but may have eternal life." The goodness of God means that he wishes to share his eternal life with us. Of course, this is our own most earnest wish. However, this cannot happen unless we *believe* in Jesus and embrace the message that he gives us. It is crucial that we understand what believing in Jesus means. It does *not* mean simply to believe that he existed or that he worked miracles and preached eloquently in Galilee. Nor does it mean to believe that he died on the cross and rose from the dead. One can accept the truth of all these statements without really changing one's life. Rather, to believe in Christ means that we accept, not only the facts about his life and death and resurrection, but also *the signifi-cance of these facts for our own lives.* In other words, we must come to understand that we need to be committed to the same *unselfish love* that we see in Jesus and that found its most per-fect expression in his dying for us on the cross. Without such a commitment, which has endless implications, it is possible to accept as true every detail of the gospel stories, and to observe all kinds of religious rituals, and still live in a selfish manner, thus effectively negating in one's own life the power of salva-tion that Jesus came to share with us.

To emphasize this point, John refers us to that strange story in the book of Numbers (21:6-9) about the bronze ser-pent that Moses placed on a pole so that those who looked upon it with faith might be delivered from a mysterious and deadly ailment. John notes the similarity between the bronze serpent lifted up for all to see and Jesus lifted up on the cross. The point to note is that the afflicted people in the desert were not cured by some magical power but by their trust in the goodness of God, who instructed Moses to act in this manner. In a similar way, all of us, who are afflicted in so many ways, are urged to see in the self-sacrifice of Jesus the ultimate sign of God's goodness and love toward us. Trusting in that good-ness and allowing it to transform our lives is the only way to eternal life.

"And this is the judgment, that the light has come into the world, and people loved darkness rather than light" (3:19)

John's Gospel is very conscious of the crisis that the com-ing of Jesus has brought into the world. This is often expressed in juridical terms as people are challenged to make a decision for or against the wisdom of Jesus. Even the Spirit is called an "Advocate" who is ready to be either a prosecuting or defense attorney for Christians who will be attacked because of their allegiance to Jesus. It may have been possible in the past to claim inculpable ignorance, but now that Jesus has come and has defined the issue so clearly, one will not be able to evade a decision. In fact, John does not hesitate to call this quite simply "the judgment" because all other human decisions pale in significance when compared with this one. The light has challenged the darkness and one can no longer live in the gray zone of indecision.

We are told that many have chosen darkness over the light "because their deeds were evil" (3:19). This statement does not explain why any reasonable persons in their right minds would do such a self-destructive thing. However, upon reflection, it becomes clear that, since the light symbolizes unselfish loving, it is only too easy to prefer the path of selfishness and darkness. It is, quite simply, so much easier to avoid the pain of truly altruistic behavior and to take instead the broad road of self-centered indulgence. Such persons "do not come to the light, so that their deeds may not be exposed" (3:20). They prefer to confuse and complicate the issue so that they may have an excuse or at least postpone their decision. Moreover, they deeply resent the witness of those who live in the light of unselfish love because this makes it so much more difficult for them to claim that what Jesus asks is far beyond the ability of fragile human beings.

By contrast, those "who do what is true come to the light, so that it may be clearly seen that their deeds have been done in God" (3:21). Just as those who want to live selfishly hate the light because it exposes their sinfulness, so those who, literally, "do the truth" gladly come to the light since it gives them the assurance of their union with Jesus. To say that these "do the truth" may sound awkward, but it is another example of the primacy of the notion of truth in John's Gospel. As we have noted already, truth in John's Gospel is not just a word for reality but is rather a code word for the revelation that Jesus has brought from his Father. To do the truth means, therefore, not just to know the truth but to live in accordance with that revelation or, in other words, to know the love of the Father and to imitate the love of Jesus.

"He must increase, but I must decrease" (3:30)

Since we are still discussing the subject of baptism, it is not surprising that John the Baptist should appear once again, not as before to announce the arrival of the Messiah, but to clarify the relationship between his baptism and that of Jesus. Recent scholarship has discovered that the Baptist was a much more influential figure than was previously thought. This accounts, no doubt, for the concern manifested by all the evangelists that the disciples of the Baptist should transfer their loyalty to Jesus. Nowhere is this expressed more clearly than in this section of John's Gospel. John the Baptist is presented as one who is intent on showing that his role is completely subordinate to that of Jesus. Jesus is the bridegroom, and the day belongs to him. The Baptist has completed his mission, and it is time for him to fade from the scene.

Whether John the Baptist handled the matter so graciously in historical reality is not so clear. This self-effacing image of the Baptist does not square very well with the portrait of him in the Synoptic Gospels where he seems less than happy with Jesus' reluctance to assert himself as political messiah (cf. Luke 7:20). In any case, John the Baptist as portrayed in the Fourth Gospel serves as a perfect model for the faithful disciple of Jesus who always tries to avoid self-promotion as he witnesses to the wonderful gift of God in his life.

"He whom God has sent speaks the words of God" (3:34)

Over and over again John's Gospel insists that Jesus does not speak in his own name, but that he tells us what he has heard from his Father. This means that he is not to be assigned a place with all those other human debaters and philosophers who offer opinions about the meaning of our existence. His witness is unique; it comes from God and carries the authority of divinity. He has not come to argue but to announce. The response to his words is not, therefore, one of intellectual agreement but one of acceptance and obedience. "Whoever believes in the Son has eternal life; whoever disobeys the Son will not see life, but must endure God's wrath" (3:36). These words are not to be interpreted as a threat but as a statement of the simple truth. And those who have had an opportunity to hear the words of Jesus must consider themselves blest beyond compare.

"Jacob's well was there" (4:6)

The well was at the center of the lives of the ancient Israelites. They were shepherds, and during the hot, dry summers, the well, which tapped into ground water, was the only resource that stood between them and slow death by famine. It was also a gathering place for lonely shepherds, and sometimes they fought over the precious water, but usually it was an occasion for friendship and laughter. It was even a place where family history was made, for it was at a well that Isaac found his wife, Rebecca (Genesis 24). Therefore, when Jesus sat down by the well of Jacob in Samaria, we must be alert to the possibility of profound symbolic meaning. In particular, the reference to life-giving water connects this story with the Christian's experience of spiritual life from the waters of baptism.

The scenario is sketched in just a few words: "Jacob's well was there, and Jesus, tired out by his journey, was sitting by the well. It was about noon. A Samaritan woman came to draw water, and Jesus said to her, 'Give me a drink'" (4:6-7). Jesus has been on the road with his disciples since early morning and, as the hot sun mounts in the sky, he becomes tired and thirsty. Jacob's well is a welcome sight. The fact that it is high noon means that it is the brightest as well as the hottest time of the day. It is also time for the brilliant light of revelation. Since the disciples have gone into the village for food, Jesus is alone when the Samaritan woman comes to the well. His request for a drink, as she draws water from the well, may seem quite natural to us, but it was far from an ordinary request at that time.

"He would have given you living water" (4:10)

The woman is shocked that Jesus should speak to her: "How is it that you, a Jew, ask a drink of me, a woman of

Samaria?" (4:9). What she is really asking is, Where are you from that you do not know the rules of this place? Otherwise you would surely know that I am one of those who are condemned to social invisibility, and indeed on two counts, first because I am a woman and then because I am a Samaritan. An adult Jewish man was not supposed to speak to a woman in public, and all Jews detested and ignored the Samaritans. On a deeper level, she is sadly reminding this mysterious person from another land that power and violence are what count in the real world where humans live.

Jesus does not say, Oh, I'm sorry, I didn't know about your customs. Quite the contrary, in fact. He knows all about those terrible rules, and he has come to cancel them. It is not he that is unaware, but she needs to realize that God does not approve of these human rules that enslave others. He says to her then: "If you knew the gift of God, and who it is that is saying to you, 'Give me a drink,' you would have asked him, and he would have given you living water" (4:10). The woman is confused because Jesus does not even have a bucket for drawing water from the well. But, of course, Jesus is not talking about the stale and stagnant well water on which most people survive. He offers a new and different kind of water—water that gives life in a way that humans have never experienced before.

Jesus enhances the noontime light as he tells her: "Everyone who drinks of this water will be thirsty again, but those who drink of the water that I will give them will never be thirsty. *The water that I will give will become in them a spring of water gushing up to eternal life*" (4:13-14, emphasis added). On one level, Jesus is referring to spring water that is always fresh and bubbling. But the real contrast is, of course, between the stale well water of a diminished human life, without faith or hope, and a life where love and respect and compassion are the primary realities. He has come to transform human society so that a situation where destructive competition is the prevailing reality gives way to a life where kindness and loving care are cherished before all else.

The meaning of the fresh, cold spring water was brought home to me personally in a very memorable way. When I was about twelve years old, I fell ill with pneumonia. It was summer-time and the heat was even more oppressive because of my rising temperature. Of course, this was long before antibiotics, and my situation soon became desperate. My father felt very helpless but he wanted to do something, so I asked if he would bring me a drink of water from that spring at the far end of the farm. I remembered how refreshing it was when we were making hay in that area. He hurried to do so and, even though the water was not very cold by the time it got to me, it seemed very, very refreshing, because with the water I received also a taste of the Father's love. The "living water" that Jesus offers is not only baptismal water; it is, first and foremost, the water of loving care which he received from his Father and now offers to us. This is the presence of the Spirit who causes the water ritual to become a source of eternal life.

"Sir, give me this water" (4:15)

By now the Samaritan woman realizes that Jesus is offering her far more than water. Her eyes must have glistened as he awakened in her the dream of possible respect and dignity and freedom. It has always been the role of the prophets, God's spokespersons, to awaken the imagination of us humans so that we might dream of a world where love replaces violence. She speaks for all of us, therefore, when she says to Jesus: "Sir, give me this water, so that I may never be thirsty or have to keep coming here to draw water" (4:15). She asks to be delivered from a world of fear and frustration.

Jesus then makes a curious request of her: "Go, call your husband, and come back" (4:16). It has been customary to interpret this request as a reminder that she must acknowledge the sinfulness of her past life as a precondition for participation in the new life that Jesus offers. Although this remains a possibility, since all conversion is based on honesty, a different and very attractive interpretation is offered by Sandra Schneiders (*The*

Revelatory Text, 2nd ed., 190), who sees here a symbolic reference to the past, not of this woman, but of her fellow Samaritans. Schneiders points out that the five husbands look very much like the five false gods, whom the Samaritans worshiped according to 2 Kings 17. In this case Jesus would be challenging all Samaritans to abandon their idolatrous past and to enter the new covenant of love and forgiveness that he has come to establish.

"The true worshipers will worship the Father in spirit and truth" (4:23)

Since Jesus seems so favorably disposed toward the Samaritans, it is almost inevitable that the woman will ask him about the rival claims of Jews and Samaritans about the proper place to worship God. The Jews claimed, of course, that it was Jerusalem, but the Samaritans, barred from Jerusalem, offered sacrifices on Mount Gerizim in Samaria. Jesus declares that Jerusalem has been the preferred place but, in the imminent messianic age, the place of worship will be relatively unimportant. What will count then is the quality of one's worship. As Ignace de la Potterie points out, the new worship will be animated by the Holy Spirit, who will enable the one who worships to be identified with Christ who is the fullness of truth, i.e., the ultimate and only adequate word of revelation (*La Vérité dans Saint Jean,* 673ff.). In fact, the new and perfect temple will be the body of the risen Lord (2:19-21). And the new worship will be profoundly trinitarian, since it will be offered to the Father, in union with the Son and at the prompting of the Spirit. This does not mean that church buildings and rituals are unimportant, for we are incarnate beings and will always need to express our worship in incarnate ways, but it does mean that the spiritual depth and quality of our worship will be far more important than any other factor.

"We know that this is truly the Savior of the world" (4:42)

The Samaritan woman becomes an effective apostle as she tells her villagers about Jesus. In this way, she shows that her conversion has been authentic, for she manifests the same zeal that Jesus himself displayed when he told his disciples, "My food is to do the will of him who sent me and to complete his work. . . . But I tell you, look around you, and see how the fields are ripe for harvesting" (4:34-35). She clearly demonstrates that it is impossible to keep such good news to oneself, and there is another feature of her witnessing that is noteworthy. She tells her villagers twice, in 4:29 and again in verse 39, that Jesus "told me everything that I have ever done." This seems to imply that the goodness of Jesus is so evident that he has been able to break through her defenses with the result that she trusts him without reserve. This tells us a great deal about the victory of real faith in a world that prizes autonomy and fears vulnerability.

In her relationship with Jesus, the Samaritan woman illustrates also the progressive steps by which the believer comes to a full recognition of the meaning of the coming of Jesus. Ignace de la Potterie sketches the steps: First, she knows Jesus only as a Jew (4:9), then as one perhaps greater than Jacob (v. 12), then as a prophet (v. 19), then as the Messiah (vs. 25-26) and, finally, as the Savior of the world (v. 42) (*La Vérité dans Saint Jean*, 683–4). This movement toward an ever more personal relationship with Jesus is a dominant feature of John's Gospel where there are constant warnings about a superficial and merely external show of Christian faith. We will see a similar progression in the story of the cure of a man born blind in John 9.

"Go; your son will live" (4:50)

The cure of the royal official's son seems to be connected to the discussion of baptism because it happens without any immediate or physical contact with Jesus. In the context, Jesus complains that people are attracted only by his miracles, whereas the important thing is the acceptance of his wisdom about how to live properly, that is, unselfishly. They are still impressed more by external signs than by the spiritual meaning of these signs. The same danger appears when the visible sign of the water ritual in baptism is taken to be what matters rather than the deep conversion that it signifies.

It is the faith of the royal official that is important. "The man believed the word that Jesus spoke to him and started on his way" (4:50), and when he found that his faith was rewarded by the cure of his son, "he himself believed, along with his whole household" (4:53). This reminder seems to be especially relevant today when so many are baptized in infancy and seldom really come to a personal awareness of the commitment that their sponsors made in their name. For what is truly operative in this sacrament is the faith that recognizes the goodness of God and that accepts the challenge to display the same kind of goodness in one's own life. The visible sign is important, but it is not nearly as significant as the invisible spiritual meaning that makes it effective for salvation.

"Stand up, take your mat and walk" (5:8)

This miracle story is situated in Jerusalem at a pool called Bethesda. It was fed by underground thermal waters, which gushed up sporadically, and were beneficial for those who were able to enter the pool when the waters were still hot. A poor crippled man could never make it down to the pool in time, though he had been trying to do so for thirty-eight years. He explains his plight to Jesus who, significantly, does not help him to the water but says simply: "Stand up, take your mat and walk" (5:8). Once again, the fact that this pool contained therapeutic water connects it with baptism. But Jesus cures the crippled man without benefit of water. This would be then another example of John's emphasis on the spiritual dimension of the sacrament and serves as a warning about the danger of a magical interpretation of baptism, as if it could give salvation through the ritual acts and words alone without the essential faith commitment.

This miracle naturally attracts attention, and some are disturbed because it happens on the Sabbath. So they inquire about the identity of the miracle worker. The man who was cured did not know who he was. But, later on, Jesus found him and said: "See, you have been made well! Do not sin any more . . ." (5:14). It is clear, therefore, that his cure cannot be separated from personal conversion. This again reminds us that the decisive element in the sacrament of baptism is the faith decision. In the case of infant baptism, as we have already noted, the personal faith decision must be made whenever one reaches the required maturity. That critical decision will involve a recognition of the truth that Jesus has revealed, namely, that God loves us and that we must also love others in the same unselfish way.

"Anyone who hears my word and believes him who sent me has eternal life" (5:24)

In the remainder of chapter 5, Jesus asserts in various ways that there is an unbreakable bond between him and the Father. Everything he says and does is in obedience to the Father. This also means that the life that the Father wishes to share with us comes only through Jesus. The primary challenge on our part is to trust our instinctive recognition of the truth that Jesus teaches. There is, of course, a strong temptation to choose instead to be guided by our rational, controlling, and prideful instincts. This happens in large measure because the recognition of Jesus' wisdom demands that we forget self and think primarily of others and of their needs. It is difficult to choose such a path. Yet it is the only way to eternal life—that joyful life that a loving Father wants so much to share with his human children.

When one is unwilling to embrace the gift of faith, which enables us to trust our instinct for the truth, all the evidence that supports the claims of Jesus is distorted. Even the Scriptures will not be understood correctly and can be used against divine purposes. Many of those who heard Jesus were very familiar with Moses and the Torah, but they could not see that Moses, properly understood, bore clear witness to Jesus. "If you believed Moses, you would believe me, for he wrote about me.

But if you do not believe what he wrote, how will you believe what I say?" (5:46-47). The problem here is not one of scientific methodology in the interpretation of the Mosaic Law. Rather, it is a lack of humility and honesty in responding to the truth that is taught by Jesus and that fulfills the Law of Moses. The way of Jesus is difficult but incredibly promising; other ways are easier but do not lead to the fulfillment which John calls eternal life.

10

Eucharist

At the time John's Gospel was written, new Christians were baptized as adults and then participated immediately in the Eucharist. The Eucharist became, therefore, the third stage, after conversion and baptism, in the gradual incorporation of the Christian into the mystery of Christ. We have already noted that the sequence of subjects in John's Gospel is determined more by the experience of Christians in the late first century than by the historical events in the life of Jesus. This seems to be confirmed by the fact that John's discussion of the Eucharist— "the bread of life"—occurs, not in chapter 13 where we find the Last Supper, but already in chapter 6, immediately after his discussion of baptism. Once again, theological considerations become more important for John than historical chronology.

It is obvious that the Eucharist is the subject of John 6, but, according to Countryman, chapter 7 also belongs under this heading (*The Mystical Way in the Fourth Gospel*, 2nd ed., 50ff.). In fact, we find that, just as the Eucharist is given to satisfy our spiritual hunger, so also is the Spirit given to satisfy our spiritual thirst. "[Jesus] cried out, 'Let anyone who is thirsty come to me, and let the one who believes in me drink.' . . . Now he said this about the Spirit . . ." (7:37-39). Thus the Eucharist, as the third stage in Christian initiation, is concerned with all aspects of nourishment on the journey that takes us ever more deeply into the mystery of Christ, that is, into a way of living that is ever more generous, thoughtful, and unselfish.

"Where are we to buy bread for these people to eat?" (6:5)

John 6 is very carefully structured. It begins with two miracle stories, both of which are intended to serve as an introduction to the subject of spiritual nourishment. The first story is that of the miraculous multiplication of the loaves and fishes to feed a multitude of hungry people. This miracle story is found in all the Gospels, but John's account has several unique features. First, there is a reference to the Passover feast: "Now the Passover, the festival of the Jews, was near" (6:4). This apparently irrelevant observation will make it easier to introduce the subject of the manna or bread from heaven, which is the subject of this chapter and which was part of the story of the original Passover. Second, the gestures of Jesus are very similar to those of the priest at the liturgy of the Eucharist: "Then Jesus took the loaves, and when he had given thanks, he distributed them. . ." (6:11). Finally, John draws a much sharper contrast than the Synoptics between the bread that was first available and the bread that was multiplied by the action of Jesus.

It is twice noted that the original bread was made from barley—a bread which is coarse and used only by the poor (6:9, 13). However, this common bread becomes, after the blessing of Jesus, so precious that great care must be taken lest any of it be lost: "When they were satisfied, [Jesus] told his disciples, 'Gather up the fragments left over, so that nothing may be lost'" (6:12). We find no such concern in the Synoptics' accounts. This serves the mystical tendencies of John very well for he wants us to discover that, just beyond the coarse and commonplace features of our world, the splendor of divinity lies hidden.

"It is I; do not be afraid" (6:20)

The second miracle story by which John sets the stage for his discussion of the Eucharist is the calming of the Sea of

Galilee. "The sea became rough because a strong wind was blowing. When they had rowed about three or four miles, they saw Jesus walking on the sea and coming near the boat, and they were terrified. But he said to them, 'It is I; do not be afraid'" (6:18-20). This account of the miracle is much shorter than the Synoptics' story (cf. Mark 6:45-51), and it focuses on the contrast between the chaotic condition of the disciples and the serenity brought by Jesus.

When John tells us that Jesus reassured the frightened disciples with the words, "It is I; do not be afraid" (6:20), he wants us to be reminded of the action of God at the time of the Exodus when he delivered the Hebrew slaves from the chaos and hopelessness of Egyptian bondage. This becomes quite clear when we note that the English translation falters here, for the words "It is I" are an inadequate translation of the Greek "I am" which is, of course, the name of the God of Exodus (Exod 3:14). John frequently uses this sacred name in reference to Jesus in order to show how he makes present the love and power of God for the liberation of all humankind (e.g., 8:58: "Very truly, I tell you, before Abraham was, I am"). From a more existential biblical perspective, this phrase means: "I am here." That is why there is no need to be afraid.

Accordingly, this miracle story, by reminding us of the liberating action of the God of Exodus, also prepares us to hear about the manna from heaven, which was a sign of God's continuous presence to his people on the difficult journey through the wilderness. These two miracle stories are, therefore, stories with a purpose, for they introduce the subject of spiritual nourishment, particularly during Israel's faith journey toward the Promised Land.

"Do not work for the food that perishes, but for the food that endures for eternal life" (6:27)

The miracle of the multiplication of loaves and fishes causes the crowd to look for Jesus and, when they find him, they call him "Rabbi" (6:25), a title that sets the stage for teaching. Jesus questions their motives but, nonetheless, does in fact begin to teach them about what constitutes authentic and lasting nourishment. He is able to offer this food because "it is on him that God the Father has set his seal" (6:27). In normal usage, a seal guarantees the authenticity of a document thus stamped. In this case Jesus refers to a special consecration that he has received from his heavenly Father, which guarantees the authenticity of his revolutionary teaching about unselfish loving.

Ultimately, the nourishment that Jesus offers is that truth to which his whole life has been dedicated, namely, the revelation, first, of the Father's unconditional love for us and, second, of our obligation and opportunity to offer, as much as possible, the same unconditional love to others. We will soon see that this is the real meaning of the Eucharist, which is all about God's love for us and of our love for others. As such, it is an epitome of the meaning of Jesus' life and teaching.

"This is the work of God, that you believe in him whom he has sent" (6:29)

The crowd asks Jesus about the "works" that God expects of his faithful followers. We can only make a guess about what they might have had in mind but, in the light of John's basic concerns, it would probably be the practice of certain ritual acts or the profession of traditional religious formulas. It is precisely to warn against such superficial religious practices that John defines the work that God expects of us in other terms. First and foremost, the work assigned to us by God is to *"believe* in him whom he has sent" (6:29, emphasis added).

As we noted earlier in regard to baptism, this means much more than believing that Jesus existed and died and rose for us. Accepting that fact is praiseworthy but does not yet satisfy the requirements of authentic faith. The critical moment in believing occurs when we accept as the guiding principle of our lives that love that caused Jesus to die for us and which alone will enable us to participate in his final victory. To believe in this sense means to become a loving, caring person in all the circumstances of life—a possibility that presupposes our personal discovery of God's love for us.

"I am the bread of life" (6:35)

The crowd ignores what Jesus has said about faith; they are not listening because they have their own agenda. They want him to provide another miraculous sign. They are more interested in spectacular phenomena than in personal conversion. Very conveniently, however, they suggest that Jesus give them a sign, which would be comparable to the manna that was miraculously provided for their ancestors in the desert. Jesus follows up on that suggestion by telling them that there is, in fact, a new manna, which is given by his heavenly Father. He tells them, "Very truly, I tell you, it was not Moses who gave you the bread from heaven, but it is my Father who gives you the true bread from heaven" (6:32). Jesus is not denying that Moses gave them manna; he simply wishes to make it clear that the gift that Moses gave them pales in significance when compared to the nourishment that is now offered by his Father.

What is this new bread from heaven which "gives life to the world" (6:33)? "Jesus said to them, 'I am the bread of life. Whoever comes to me will never be hungry, and whoever believes in me will never be thirsty'" (6:35). Jesus is himself the gift of God that provides nourishment for all who are on the journey of faith. Raymond Brown is surely right in warning us not to assume immediately that Jesus is referring here to his Body and Blood in the Eucharist. Rather, in verses 35-50, the term should be taken in the sense it has in the Wisdom literature of the Hebrew Scriptures, namely, that the bread from heaven is God's *revelation*. It is God's nourishing word which, when accepted and lived, becomes a source of life. Brown writes: "The fundamental reaction to Jesus' presentation of himself as bread in 35-50 is that of belief (35, 36, 40, 47) or of coming to him, which is a synonym for belief (35, 37, 44, 47)" (*The Gospel according to John*, vol. 1, 273). At this stage, therefore, Jesus is the bread from heaven as the truth or wisdom that will give us life if we embrace it with faith.

Two examples from the Hebrew Scriptures illustrate this meaning of bread from heaven. In Proverbs, Lady Wisdom invites all to come to her banquet: "Come, eat of my bread and drink of the wine I have mixed" (9:5). Lady Wisdom is certainly not talking about physical food and drink; rather, she is inviting us to listen to her words of wisdom, which can nourish our spiritual life. Bread and wine are metaphors for spiritual nourishment, and in Isaiah we read: "For as the rain and snow come down from heaven, and do not return there until they have watered the earth, making it bring forth and sprout, giving seed to the sower and bread to the eater, so shall my word be that goes out from my mouth; it shall not return to me empty . . ." (55:10-11). Once again, bread is a metaphor for God's beneficent and spiritually nourishing word of revelation.

It is important to insist that Jesus, at this stage of his discourse, is referring to himself, not yet as eucharistic bread, but as the one who offers the bread or food of revelation. For it is fairly certain that John took the rather drastic step of moving the account of the institution of the Eucharist from the Last Supper to chapter 6 precisely so that he could introduce it with a lengthy discussion of the need for *faith* before one can receive the Eucharist in a fruitful manner. In other words, Jesus as the bread of life must be received in faith before he can be properly received as Eucharist. That means that his teaching of unselfish love must be accepted before one can fruitfully receive the primary sacramental expression of that love which is the Eucharist—the sacrament of his Body and Blood given for us.

We find an excellent summary of this in the words of Jesus himself: "This is indeed the will of my Father, that all who see the Son and *believe* in him may have eternal life; and I will raise them up on the last day" (6:40, emphasis added). The Father's love thus finds concrete expression in the incarnate Son with the hope that those of us who come to know Jesus and embrace his message in faith may be blest with eternal life.

If we join our unselfish loving with his, the result will be a participation in his glorious resurrection. At this point, however, the emphasis is still on our believing which is a precondition for fruitful participation in the Body and Blood of Jesus.

"Whoever believes has eternal life" (6:47)

The crowd takes exception to the words of Jesus that he is the bread from heaven. "They were saying, 'Is not this Jesus, . . . whose father and mother we know? How can he now say, "I have come down from heaven"?'" (6:42). We have already noted that John considers one of the necessary characteristics of disciples of Jesus to be that they be open to surprise (see comments on 1:46). God almost never does things exactly as we expect. The crowd cannot see beyond Jesus' human origins but, from a mystical perspective, it is precisely behind such prosaic appearances that God's special gift is to be found.

Jesus reminds both them and us that this kind of human reasoning will never discover God's gift: "No one can come to me unless drawn by the Father who sent me . . ." (6:44). It is only when we put aside our quest for human control that we can begin to feel the Father's powerful magnetism as he touches our innermost being and enables us to find in Jesus the answer to our yearning for peace and joy. It is this deep, personal commitment to Christ that must precede our approach to the sacrament of the Eucharist. Of course, this believing in him may be weak at first, but it will grow as we open ourselves to the gift of God and the Eucharist itself will help to strengthen our faith.

"The bread that I will give for the life of the world is my flesh" (6:51)

Only in John 6:51 do we find an explicit and unmistakable reference to the Eucharist as the sacrament of the Body and Blood of the Lord: "and the bread that I will give for the life of the world is my flesh." This is John's account of the institution of the Eucharist, and it contains all the essential elements of other institution accounts, whether in the Synoptics' passion narratives (Mark

14:22-24 and parallels), or in Paul's 1 Corinthians 11:24-25. Moreover, it is hard to imagine how John could have been clearer in asserting the realism of this sacramental presence. In fact, the explanatory statement of Jesus is both solemn and dramatic:

> Very truly, I tell you, unless you eat the flesh of the Son of Man and drink his blood, you have no life in you. Those who eat my flesh and drink my blood have eternal life, and I will raise them up on the last day; for my flesh is true food and my blood is true drink (6:53-55).

This statement not only means that the Body and Blood of the Lord are truly present in the Eucharist but also that this presence challenges all who receive the sacrament to make present in their lives the unselfish love that it exemplifies. In fact, it seems to be precisely this danger of reverencing the sacrament, perhaps with great scrupulosity, but neglecting its meaning in one's life, that caused John to locate the institution of the Eucharist in a context where a *believing* reception is so strongly emphasized. John seems to be exceedingly concerned lest Christian observance represent only the external practice of rituals and the recognition of titles without that personal, experiential union with Christ which alone responds adequately to his life and message.

In a contemporary setting, it is sad to note how some will place a high premium on gestures, such as genuflection, or on precise and orthodox words, important as these may be, but whose lives do not manifest the compassion and loving concern that are the essential signs of one's union with Christ. In fact, meticulous observance can actually become dangerous if it allows one to live in the illusion that this alone suffices to make one a good Christian, and it becomes a tragic illusion if it is trusted to guarantee final victory with Christ.

"Those who eat my flesh and drink my blood abide in me, and I in them" (6:56)

Having recalled the fact of the institution of the Eucharist, John now spells out some of the consequences for the believer. Sharing in the Body and Blood of Jesus creates a mystical union with him that satisfies the deepest yearnings of the human heart. The verb translated as "abide" is the same verb used in 1:38 where the disciples ask Jesus where he is staying. We noted there that this was far more than a request about his residence. Rather, it amounted to a question about where our true home is. At that point, Jesus said, "Come and see" (1:39). And now we discover that where we truly belong and where we can find peace and security is in a personal union with him through participation in his Body and Blood. Of course, we must be careful to note that this is not some magical or mechanical process. For true participation in the Body and Blood of Jesus requires a decision to live and love as he did. In other words, it means to participate in his Body broken and his Blood poured out for others.

Jesus then announces a dramatic conclusion concerning the possibility of union with him in the Eucharist: "Just as the living Father sent me, and I live because of the Father, so whoever eats me will live because of me" (6:57). It is easy to miss the radical nature of this statement. In fact, Jesus is telling us that when we mere human beings participate in his loving, made present in the Eucharist, we begin to live with the same divine life that he shares with his heavenly Father.

Raymond Brown has noted the dramatic implications of such a statement. He writes that

> in its brevity vs. 57 is a most forceful expression of the tremendous claim that Jesus gives man a share in God's own life, an expression far more real than the abstract formulation of II Pet. 1:4. And so it is that, while the Synoptic Gospels record the institution of the Eucharist, it is John who explains what the Eucharist does for the Christian (*The Gospel according to John*, vol. 1, 292–3).

The text of 2 Peter, to which Brown refers, is generally considered to be the most daring statement in the New Testament about the possibility of union between God and humans.

That text asserts that God has given "his precious and very great promises, so that through them you may . . . become participants of the divine nature" (1:4). Sharing through the Eucharist in the life that flows between the Persons of the Trinity, however, appears to be a much more vital and personal expression of the possibility of union with God.

This possibility of sharing the very life of God comes so close to pantheism that it has caused many to be frightened away from mystical experience. This is most unfortunate because mystical experience of the divine presence in one's life remains the ideal for all Christians. The danger of pantheism, which takes away one's personal identity, can be avoided if one is careful to participate in the sacramental life of the Christian community. Ideally, there should be a healthy balance between the communal and the individual experience of God's presence, and this result follows necessarily where personal union with Christ means a participation in the kind of love that the Eucharist represents. Thus, if our loving is truly unselfish, it will reach out to community and will want to avoid any extreme forms of individual piety.

"This teaching is difficult; who can accept it?" (6:60)

The "word" or "teaching" to which this text refers is often thought to be the emphatic statement by Jesus concerning the *reality* of his Body and Blood in the Eucharist. This conclusion is very doubtful, however, especially if one pays attention to the context. In fact, when Jesus responds to this objection, he does not reaffirm the reality of his eucharistic presence but, after noting his authority as one coming from the transcendent world, he states: "It is the spirit that gives life; the flesh is useless. The words that I have spoken to you are spirit and life" (6:63). This would be a very strange way to reaffirm the reality of his flesh and blood in the Eucharist. But it makes very good sense if Jesus is reasserting the validity of his primary teaching—the ultimate truth—that we must join him in his unselfish loving. Upon reflection, it is clear that the most difficult teaching of Jesus is his demand that we live unselfishly. The "flesh" to which Jesus refers, then, would be a code word for selfishness, as it is in the writings of St. Paul, just as the "spirit" stands for unselfishness (see Gal 5:16-26).

I do not suggest for a moment, of course, that reverence for the sacrament is unimportant. But it must be obvious that more than that is required. Perhaps the point can be illustrated by a possible scenario drawn from a monastic setting. I can well imagine a young novice going to church to kneel before the Blessed Sacrament when he should be at recreation with his confreres. He might even think that this could help him to achieve that reputation for holiness that he seeks so earnestly. In this case, I would not be surprised if Jesus opened the door of the tabernacle and told him, ever so gently, My friend, don't you know that I offered myself for others? Don't you know that this is what the Eucharist really means? By all means, come to visit me again, but your place now is with your confreres who need your presence and your love!

"Lord, to whom can we go?" (6:68)

We are told that many of Jesus' followers were frightened away by his teaching about the need to love unselfishly. Their cultural environment and their own experience have told them insistently that they must take care of themselves rather than trust in their sacrifices for others. It is just too difficult to move away from such a "sensible" approach to life. Thus Jesus turns to his immediate disciples, to those Twelve who have shared his life and who have received his daily instructions, and he asks them: "Do you also wish to go away?" (6:67).

Peter takes the lead, as usual, and gives Jesus a rather curious answer: "Lord, to whom can we go?" (6:68). This is hardly the kind of ringing endorsement that one would expect from the prince of the apostles. It seems that Peter is saying, We wish we could change things, but we have gone too far with you and only our love can now save us from the infidelity that our reason would counsel. Anyone who has loved and trusted another person will probably experience moments of doubt and regret, but if that love is more than infatuation, it will survive such hesitations. In fact, Peter seems to confirm this interpretation when he says, "We have come to believe and know that you are the Holy One of God" (6:69). In other words, our love and trust have grown, day by day, and now it is much too late to turn back.

The chapter ends on a somber note because it is necessary to point out that one of those intimate Twelve will in fact betray his master. Jesus says: "Did I not choose you, the twelve? Yet one of you is a devil" (6:70). The Greek word for "devil" means literally a "deceiver," and it seems accurate to say that Judas was in fact living a lie. It is impossible to know the interior thoughts and motives of Judas, but it does seem that he was not able to come to the kind of love for Jesus that prevented Peter and the others from defecting. One has the impression that Judas loved the project that Jesus seemed to be promoting—a political agenda of power and glory—but he could not come to a personal love that would remain even when it became clear that Jesus had no interest in that project. Love for projects, no matter how sublime, will never survive the hardships of life; only love of persons can do that.

"Now the Jewish festival of Booths was near" (7:2)

Chapter 7 continues the theme of Eucharist because, during the celebration of the feast of Booths, or Tabernacles, Jesus declares publicly that he has come to satisfy those who are thirsty (7:37). Thus the theme of spiritual nourishment is continued, but this climax is reached only after a lengthy introduction. The feast of Booths was a major Jewish feast, which required all adults to make a pilgrimage to Jerusalem. The feast itself was a joyous occasion corresponding to our Thanksgiving Day. It celebrated the grape harvest, which explains why they gathered in booths or temporary shelters erected in the vineyards where there would be drinking and singing and dancing. More elaborate religious ceremonies would take place in Jerusalem.

The disciples want Jesus to go with them to Jerusalem for this feast, but he declines and then does go secretly. There is no question of deception here but simply a refusal to go in the way the disciples wish, that is, to declare his messianic intentions in the capital city. Jesus knows that Jerusalem will not be the place of his political debut but rather the place where he will be revealed as the Savior by dying for others. This kind of public sacrifice will reveal the love of the Father and the truth about the meaning and purpose of our existence. The story develops on two levels: many are discussing and arguing about his messianic possibilities, whereas he wants to talk about loving and dying.

"Jesus went up into the temple and began to teach" (7:14)

Jesus dares to enter the temple precincts and to begin teaching there. This causes amazement because he talks like a learned rabbi, but there is no evidence that he has had a prominent teacher as was normal for rabbis. This allows Jesus to declare once again that his learning comes from his contact with God. He notes, moreover, that this will be evident to anyone "who resolves to do the will of God" (7:17). In other words, the validity of his message will be determined, not by checking out his academic credentials but by an intuitive recognition of his completely unselfish motivation. He continues, "Those who speak on their own seek their own glory; but the one who seeks the glory of him who sent him is true, and there is nothing false in him" (7:18). Such intuitive recognition does not come from human effort, but from having a heart that is responsive to the will of God, that is, a heart that is filled with the loving that is natural to God and is revealed in Jesus.

Jesus then presses the issue by pointing out their hypocrisy in being scandalized because he has healed on the Sabbath and, at the same time, claiming to be disciples of Moses. They fail to understand that the Law of Moses makes full provision for religious acts, such as circumcision, on the Sabbath. The problem is not, therefore, with the Law of Moses but with their rigid, human interpretation of that Law. Some also question his messianic credentials because he comes from Nazareth, a place that has never had messianic pretensions. Jesus trumps their human wisdom by declaring that he comes from God: "I know him, because I am from him, and he sent me" (7:29). All other considerations are irrelevant. There is something very sad about this situation where humans try to measure and control divine mystery with the tragic result that they risk losing both the mystery and its splendid gift, which alone can give them the happiness they seek.

"Let anyone who is thirsty come to me, and let the one who believes in me drink" (7:37-38)

John tells us that Jesus "cried out" these words on the final and climactic day of the great festival at Jerusalem. It is scarcely possible to overestimate their importance. Moreover, the contention that these words continue the theme of the Eucharist seems confirmed by the words of Jesus that follow: "As the Scripture says, 'Out of his heart shall flow rivers of living water'" (7:38, author's translation). One searches in vain for such a text in the Hebrew Scriptures. However, as Raymond Brown points out, the reference is almost certainly to the Exodus story about Moses who produced water in the desert by striking the rock at God's command (Exod 17:6). This episode is also echoed in Psalm 78:16 where Moses is said to have "made streams come out of the rock. . . ." Also in Psalm 105:40-41, we read: "[He] gave them food from heaven in abundance. He opened the rock, and water gushed out . . . ." Brown comments: "This sequence of bread from heaven and water from the rock is exactly the sequence we have in chs. vi and vii of John . . ." (*The Gospel according to John*, vol. 1, 322). It is surely legitimate, therefore, to view chapter 7 as a continuation of John's discussion of the Eucharist, for the "living water" that Jesus offers does for the thirsty exactly what the "bread of life" does for the hungry.

John then offers an intriguing comment on the words of Jesus about the gift of living water: "Now he said this about the

Spirit, which believers in him were to receive; for as yet there was no Spirit, because Jesus was not yet glorified" (7:39). This statement clearly reflects a post-resurrection awareness and it clarifies the situation of the Johannine community. They have been experiencing the presence of the Holy Spirit who has helped them to penetrate more deeply into the message of Jesus and thus to remain faithful in a time of persecution.

It is precisely this message of Jesus that is promised to the Samaritan woman under the imagery of "living water" (4:10). This living water is, therefore, the teaching or revelation of Jesus, which offers life to all who embrace it in faith and live it fully. Moreover, the revelation that Jesus brings to us from the Father is the truth for which Jesus came into this world (18:37). As we noted earlier in chapter 5, this fuller revelation offered by the Spirit is the knowledge of how to apply the command of unselfish loving to every circumstance of life. Thus, this ideal of unselfishness, which is embodied, as it were, in the Eucharist, is also the meaning of the living, refreshing water of the Spirit.

"Never has anyone spoken like this!" (7:46)

The words of Jesus produce animated discussion among the people who hear him. They yearn for a Messiah, and he seems to come tantalizingly close to satisfying their aspirations. However, they apply standards that are too political and too human. They cannot understand that Jesus is breaking out of all the old structures and is challenging them to let God start something entirely new. Their problem is similar to that of people who define happiness so narrowly that they cannot receive it even when it is offered to them. Once again, it is worth remembering that the best gifts in life are the ones we do not control and cannot anticipate.

The temple police who are sent to arrest Jesus come close to recognizing what is at stake when they fail in their efforts and explain to their superiors that it is because "Never has anyone spoken like this!" (7:46). The words of Jesus reach them at a level that is beyond rational constructs and traditional prejudices. But the religious authorities, who trust control and human wisdom more than openness to the transcendent world, scold them for their apparent gullibility: "Surely you have not been deceived too, have you? Has any of the authorities or of the Pharisees believed in him? But this crowd, which does not know the law—they are accursed" (7:47-48). How tragically ironic! The very ones who do know something about the Law of Moses find that their desire to control that Law has made it impossible for them to see that it was really meant to prepare them for something more surprising and wonderful than they had ever imagined.

We need to remember, once again, that passages such as this tell us more about the situation in the community of John at the end of the first century than it does about the ministry of Jesus. For the Johannine community, with its mystical appreciation of the divinity of Jesus and the presence of the Spirit among them, is frustrated beyond measure by the stubborn resistance that they experience when they offer this wisdom to their friends and neighbors. These would include not only their fellow Jews, who have not accepted Jesus, but also some other Christians who are fearful and skeptical about the mystical dimension of religion. The same problem exists today, although we would express it in different terms. For the scientific study of revelation is not meant to clear up all its mysteries but should lead us to a recognition of the depth of the divine mystery and to prepare us for worship. Once again, good theology is intended to help us locate the Mystery, not to eliminate it.

The final words of John 7 signal the end of this discussion of the bread of life and the living water: "Then each of them went home" (7:53). And so we are invited to proceed with John to the next stage, which will take us into the uniquely Johannine realm of mystical enlightenment.

11

Enlightenment

Enlightenment represents the fourth stage in the movement of the believer from conversion, through baptism and
Eucharist, to an ever deeper mystical union with God in Christ.
Arrival at this stage is signaled by the dramatic statement of
Jesus: "I am the light of the world" (8:12), used here for the first
time in the Gospel. We know that mystical writers often describe
their experience as an enlightenment. It is as if the mysterious,
spiritual side of life has suddenly been illuminated in a way that
provides a clear vision of all that is essential in human life.

From a biblical perspective, this experience would be the
discovery in one's life of the luminous cloud that appeared to
the Israelites after their liberation from Egypt. As a cloud, it
stands for mystery, but it is not the dark mystery of chaos, but
the luminous reality of a mystical understanding that is more
real that any rational comprehension. The cloud is therefore
filled with light. This mystical discovery also illuminates the
future, just as the luminous cloud of Exodus guided the Israelites toward the Promised Land:

> The Lord went in front of them in a pillar of cloud by day, to
> lead them along the way, and in a pillar of fire by night, to give
> them light, so that they might travel both by day and by night.

Neither the pillar of cloud by day nor the pillar of fire by night left its place in front of the people (Exod 13:21-22).

This illumination of the future enables one to overcome fear of the unknown as one comes to realize that the future is filled with the promise of a loving God who prepares a wonderful home for us. Thus, fear and anxiety gradually give way to joyful anticipation.

We have concluded that John, in these early chapters, simply interweaves the story of Jesus' public ministry with the experience of believers who move through the various stages of Christian initiation. Having reached the climax of this process in reception of the Eucharist, they are now invited to make their religious experience more profound and personal by a mystical enlightenment. L. William Countryman notes the significance of this moment from John's perspective: "In this section of the Gospel, our author moves beyond the external forms of membership in the Christian community and deals with aspects of believing that have no clear or invariable external indications. Enlightenment cannot be certified by fulfillment of a rite" (*The Mystical Way in the Fourth Gospel*, 2nd ed., 66). This is a critical moment in the lives of Christians because it challenges them to go beyond the external (and perhaps superficial) observance of rituals and recitation of prayers to a truly personal union with God. Such enlightenment occurs only when one's experience of conversion, baptism, and Eucharist reaches a certain depth or achieves a certain maturity.

"I am the light of the world" (8:12)

Jesus does not make this dramatic announcement so that we, who struggle with darkness, may simply admire him, but rather that we may follow him into the realm of light. For he continues: "Whoever follows me will never walk in darkness but will have the light of life" (8:12). We know from other Johannine texts that to walk in the darkness means to lead a sinful life, just as walking in the light means to love as Jesus does (cf., e.g., 3:19-20 and 13:34).

To the extent that we are able to love unselfishly, there-fore, we will move from the darkness of a self-centered life to the light of loving concern and compassion. As this happens, we will realize that the external elements in our religious ob-servance were always intended merely to lead us to this ideal condition and to aid us in remaining there. Their presence in our lives will always be important but they are only a means, not an end in themselves. Following the luminous cloud will be a journey into the depths of an ever stronger love and an ever closer union with God. By that very fact, it will also mean a deeper mystical union with God in Christ.

"The Father who sent me testifies on my behalf" (8:18)

The Pharisees react strongly to Jesus' claim to be the light of the world. They point out that he is testifying in his own be-half and that his claims are, therefore, entirely gratuitous. They are quite right, of course, from a purely human or juridical standpoint. But Jesus has not come to argue juridical positions. He has come to offer them the assurance of God's love in a way that they have never known before. Requiring proof of this is like children asking their parents to prove that they love them. And, in a sense, this is exactly the analogy that Jesus draws upon when he says: "I testify on my own behalf, and the Father who sent me testifies on my behalf" (8:18). In other words, Jesus can testify to his own experience of the Father's love, and he can invite others to open their hearts to that love. When they do so, there will be no further need of testimony.

The basic problem is not with the validity of Jesus' claim but with the lack of trust on the part of those, whose lives he offers to illuminate. They cannot let go of the need to control and evaluate, whereas what Jesus offers is precisely a love that is not subject to control and human evaluation. It is like ask-ing someone to prove that he is not lying. Our Western cul-ture, especially since the Enlightenment, has become so rationalist that trust is often demeaned to the status of gul-libility. Yet, in matters of the spirit, trust is the only way to break out of this doomed material world into the spiritual world of ultimate liberation and fulfillment.

"Then they said to him, 'Where is your Father?' Jesus answered, 'You know neither me nor my Father. If you knew me, you would know my Father also'" (8:19). In all likelihood, those who ask Jesus about the identity of his father are thinking of his human father, who is perhaps a person of note whose testimony would carry some weight on the human level. Jesus can only point out once again that he himself, with his personal witness to love and compassion, is the only one through whom they will ever come to know his heavenly Father, source of all love and all goodness. We can only begin to feel the frustration and sadness of Jesus whose offer of the ultimate gift is received with a demand for proof. Once again, we must note that Jesus stands here for the Johannine community also. For they wish to tell others about the wonderful mystical experience that they have discovered only to be rebuffed and despised for their efforts.

John tells us that Jesus bore witness to the love of his Father in "the treasury of the temple" (8:20), that is, in the very center of that religious establishment that could not open itself to his message. However, "no one arrested him, because his hour had not yet come" (8:20). This surprising fact is surely intended to show that, though Jesus will eventually succumb to evil human machinations, the timetable for salvation is always and everywhere in the hands of God. In spite of appearances at any given moment, the love of God will conquer all evil and violence in the end. No matter how dark the valley in which we dwell may become, the horizon will always be illuminated by God's promise. The light will conquer the darkness.

"For you will die in your sins unless you believe that I am he" (8:24)

Jesus has just told his audience that he is going away, and they will not be able to find him. They wonder whether he is perhaps going to kill himself. Jesus explains: "Where I am going, you cannot come" (8:21). No, he is not going to kill himself; it is just that he is going to this other world to which they have no access by their own means. "You are from below, I am from above; you are of this world, I am not of this world" (8:23). Of course, God did not mean for us to be stuck in this world where death has the last word. But when we refuse to open our hearts to the message that Jesus brings, and when we persist in the sinfulness of selfish behavior and turn our backs on the world of light and life, we condemn ourselves to darkness and death. That is what Jesus means when he warns them, "I am going away, and you will search for me, but you will die in your sin" (8:21). To live in the darkness is to condemn oneself to the tragedy of a fruitless search.

Then Jesus tells them (and us) how to avoid that dreadful fate: "you will die in your sins unless you believe that I AM" (8:24, author's translation). The English, "I am he," simply does not convey the deeper biblical meaning of the Greek, "I am." And, as we have noted elsewhere, this takes us back to the classic text of Exodus 3:14, where the God who delivers the Hebrew slaves from bondage identifies himself as "I AM." When God tells Moses that "I AM" is the name of the God who will deliver the Hebrew slaves from bondage, he is not affirming simply that he exists but that he is present and wishes to help. The Hebrews had no real interest in theoretical existence. Jesus defines himself, therefore, as one in whom the God of Exodus is present and willing to save once again. He is, as it were, the extension into our world of this power of God to love and save. And when Jesus says that we will die in our sins unless we believe that he is "I AM," he is declaring that the only way to escape final death is to trust the power of God that he offers. We do this by believing in him.

The people listening to Jesus are sufficiently intrigued by this statement to ask, "Who are you?" (8:25). With a sigh, Jesus tells them again that he is the one sent from heaven. Moreover, "the one who sent me is true, and I declare to the world what I have heard from him" (8:26). In other words, I am the one who brings you that ultimate truth which I have known in heaven and which I bring to earth. That saving truth is, of course, that God loves you and that you should love one another. Everything else is relatively untrue. Jesus makes this clear when he returns to the dramatic claim to be "I AM": "When you have lifted up the Son of Man, then you will realize that I AM . . ." (8:28, author's translation). This lifting up of Jesus in his crucifixion will be the ultimate proof of God's love for us: "For God so loved the world that he gave his only Son, so that everyone who believes in him may not perish but may have eternal life" (3:16).

To believe in Jesus as the sign and proof of God's love for us is to be liberated by that love for loving service to others. This is so true that, if our lives are not in fact filled with loving concern for others, it is proof positive that we have not really allowed the love of God to penetrate to the center of our being.

"If you continue in my word, you are truly my disciples" (8:31)

This statement of Jesus is addressed to "the Jews who had believed in him" (8:31). The obvious implication is that some of those Jews who had heard Jesus identify himself with the loving and liberating God of Exodus were won over by his witnessing and had taken the first step of initial belief in him. Jesus recognizes the tentative nature of their commitment and invites them to "continue" in his word. This word is, of course, the revelation—the truth—that he brings from the Father. It is not a message that can be embraced quickly and easily, and that is why Jesus urges them to continue on their journey of faith to an ever-deeper appreciation of what this message entails.

This "continuing in his word" is far more than merely persevering in that initial, still tentative kind of faith that they have achieved. For the verb "to continue" is in fact a rendering of the Greek word that is usually translated "to abide" or "to remain." As we know by now, this is one of John's favorite words, and it is often used to describe the intimate union between the Persons of the Trinity as well as the mystical union of the believer with God (see 15:5-11). What Jesus asks of these tentative believers is, therefore, that they stay with him so that gradually the vision and the direction of their lives may change. Thus they will become evermore united with him in his unconditional love—a love that is possible because of the experienced goodness of the Father. In this way alone will Jesus be able to call them "truly my disciples" (8:31). Once again, we note John's deep concern about the danger of a superficial and merely external practice of religion. We should note also that being a believer for a long time is no guarantee that one's faith has ceased to be superficial!

"You will know the truth, and the truth will make you free" (8:32)

The above text is indeed a golden text and, in my estimation, one of the most important statements in the entire Gospel of John. The true disciple is the one who "abides" in the word of Jesus. Such a one doesn't just hear his message but also dwells with it, cherishes it, embraces it gladly, accepts its challenge, and is nourished by its wisdom. Such a one will also learn that this word is Jesus himself so that, as one savors the precious word, it will gradually blend into the even more precious person of the Lord. This will also mean living with, and making one's own, that truth for which Jesus was born and for which he came into this world (18:37)—a truth that became incarnate in his dying for us.

In this way, the dedicated believer will gradually come to "know" the truth. This is far more than having an intellectual grasp of the truth of some statement or equation. It is that rich biblical concept of knowing that involves a profound acceptance that engages the whole person. The freedom that comes from such a personal welcome of Jesus' word is an inner freedom, a deep sense of confidence, and the peace that comes from having found where one truly belongs. This kind of freedom cannot be taken away, not by violence and not even by death. It is a creature finding its creator as a sliver of steel finds and locks onto a magnet.

Those Jews who have begun to believe do not respond positively to Jesus' invitation to deepen their faith. Instead, they turn combative and take offense at his suggestion that they are still in some kind of bondage. "We are descendants of Abraham and have never been slaves to anyone" (8:33). Being afraid to follow the path into mystery and obedience that Jesus offers them, they make the fateful decision to retreat to the more familiar territory of their vaunted privileges as descendants of Abraham. Unfortunately, however, this is an Abraham with whom they have become familiar only by overlooking his radical obedience to the mysterious and demanding word of God in his life. But now, even that word of God to Abraham has been superceded by the ultimate Word, which is the Son of God made flesh: "So if the Son makes you free you will be free indeed" (8:36). The new word is always more challenging than the old, familiar word; but it is only the new word demanding conversion that gives life.

"If God were your Father, you would love me" (8:42)

Jesus challenges their appeal to Abraham. They cannot be children of Abraham if they are not open to God's mysterious word just as Abraham was. And, in that case, they are not even children of God. In fact, they cannot recognize the word that comes from God and offers them life. Their desire to control and to be on "safe" ground prevents them from trusting their innate readiness for God's revelation, and the consequence is disastrous. For failure to recognize the truth means that one is condemned to live in deception and illusion—and that is, of course, the realm of the great deceiver, Satan. Jesus continues:

> Why do you not understand what I say? It is because you cannot accept my word. You are from your father the devil, and you choose to do your father's desires. He was a murderer from the beginning and does not stand in the truth, because there is no truth in him. When he lies, he speaks according to his own nature, for he is a liar and the father of lies (8:43-44).

The word "devil" comes from the Greek word for "deceiver." The devil offers us humans the big lie, that human success and happiness can be achieved through selfish concern for one's own interests with no regard for the needs of others. Because this view is so appealing from a merely rational assessment, it constitutes a temptation that is almost irresistible. By contrast, Jesus offers them (and us) the difficult but life-giving truth: "because I tell the truth, you do not believe me" (8:45). The logic is unassailable: "Whoever is from God hears the words of God. The reason you do not hear them is that you are not from God" (8:47). Whether we are "from God" is not a matter of luck but of choice. We are meant to be from God, but we are also free to choose a way that seems to us more promising. Tragically, we are free to commit suicide.

"Now we know that you have a demon" (8:52)

The language on both sides of this issue is strong and personal. That is because there is so much at stake. It has even been suggested that this whole chapter should be deleted from the New Testament since it has been appealed to by those who, over the years, have engaged in the worst kind of anti-Semitism. A much wiser course is to work patiently and persistently for a proper interpretation of these passages. If Jesus accuses some of being children of the devil, it is certainly not because they are Jews. After all, he himself and his disciples are Jews. Rather, he is challenging those *of any race or time* who close their eyes to the life-giving truth that he offers. The language is strong also because it reflects the frustration of the Johannine community with all those who rebuff their efforts to share their mystical insights. We must keep in mind, here also, that the text should be read on the level of both the ministry of Jesus and the experience of John's community in the 80s and 90s.

Jesus is said to have a demon because it is a classic procedure to demonize a challenge that one cannot refute but does not wish to accept. The particular focus of their accusation is the claim of Jesus that he offers a life that even Abraham and the prophets did not enjoy (8:53). Such a claim forces them either to acknowledge his divine origins or to judge him a blasphemer. As we shall see in the story of the blind man, which follows in John 9 and illustrates this dilemma, they cannot recognize his divine origins without giving up their own control in the area of determining right and wrong. John's Gospel is all about how Jesus clarifies issues so that one must choose and is thus exposed to judgment. That could not be clearer than in this section of his Gospel. The word of Jesus brings light and life; those who reject it choose darkness and death.

Chapter 8 ends with a declaration by Jesus that highlights his divinity in a way that we never see in the Synoptic Gospels. Jesus has just claimed that their great patriarch Abraham rejoiced to see his day, no doubt because he delighted in contemplating the promise of God. Refusing to move beyond the human plane, Jesus' antagonists accuse him of claiming more than is his right: "You are not yet fifty years old, and have you seen Abraham?" (8:57). To which Jesus replies, "Very truly, I tell you, before Abraham was, I AM" (8:58, author's translation). The supreme God of Exodus, who called Israel into being, is present now in Jesus to call all of us to ultimate freedom and life. The decision to respond generously to this call is the most important decision we will ever make . . . and all our happiness depends upon it.

"He saw a man blind from birth" (9:1)

All of chapter 9 is devoted to the story of Jesus' cure of a man born blind. Actually, only a few verses of this lengthy chapter are concerned with the cure itself. Most of the chapter deals with the symbolic significance of this act of Jesus, and that means that it is concerned with enlightenment. The blind man represents all of us who are called out of darkness by the word of Jesus. In fact, the cure of this man's physical blindness is only the beginning of his recovery. For he must overcome his spiritual blindness also. By contrast, the Pharisees, who begin with physical sight, end up in spiritual darkness.

The disciples pose an old question for Jesus: "Rabbi, who sinned, this man or his parents, that he was born blind?" (9:2).

The spiritual leaders of that time spent days in discussing this kind of issue. Jesus is impatient with this kind of fruitless debate. "Neither this man nor his parents sinned; he was born blind so that God's works might be revealed in him" (9:3). In other words, God's goodness and mercy must be offered to this poor man here and now. Arguing about the origin of his plight does not help him. The Johannine community is tired of such endless debates also, for they leave the world unchanged.

"As long as I am in the world, I am the light of the world" (9:5)

Jesus is ready to move from futile debate to merciful action. In this way he will show that God's light has come into the world to dispel the darkness of self-centered behavior. For he then demonstrates that being "the light of the world" means making the plight of a poor blind man one's own concern. Through sympathy, he identifies with this man, making room in his life for him. He anoints the blind man's eyes with a mixture of spittle and soil, perhaps symbolizing the word of revelation applied to the soil of needy humanity, and sends him to the pool of Siloam, interpreted as "Sent," which is a code word for Jesus, sent from the Father. The effect is immediate and dramatic: "Then he went and washed and came back able to see" (9:7).

The neighbors are amazed at the change in him. Some wonder even whether it is the same person. But he bears witness: "I am the man" (9:9). Then they ask what happened and he tells them that "the man called Jesus" (9:11) has cured him. At this point he does not know Jesus except by hearsay, for he was still blind when he was last in his presence. This represents the first stage of faith when we believe because of the witness of parents or other influential persons. In this childhood experience, we come to know about the reality and goodness of God or Jesus because those whom we trust tell us that it is so. In a very real sense we believe with the faith of our parents. This is the way it should be for children, but when we leave childhood, our faith must grow also. If it does not, we will have no choice but to answer as the former blind man does when they ask where Jesus is: "He said, 'I do not know'" (9:12).

"He is a prophet" (9:17)

At this stage the Pharisees are brought into the picture. They are known for their strict observance of the Law, but it is an observance that is too human and too rigid. They seem to have forgotten that the supreme law is the command to love and that all other laws must be subordinate to that law. We all find it very hard to remember this because, when we give primacy to the law of love, we can no longer control our lives as we would like. For we never know where loving concern for others will lead us. The Pharisees in this story illustrate this truth perfectly, for they are incensed to discover that Jesus has cured the blind man on a Sabbath. Their controlling instincts tell them that this cannot be a miracle because God would never give power to one who performs a "sinful" act. Yet their common sense tells them that one could never do such an act without God's assistance.

Jesus could easily have chosen to perform this miracle on some other day, but he feels obliged to confront and expose the fallacy of their religious reasoning. Responding to the need of this blind man is surely more virtuous than observing a law that has become too rigid. In this case, the law must bend, not the poor blind man. This does not mean that laws are to be despised, for we need the order that they bring to our lives. However, this human order, if it is not subordinated to the divine order of love and mercy, will soon become tyranny. It is important to remember that there was much "law and order" in the pharaoh's Egypt (and in many oppressive regimes since then), but it benefited only the elite. In contrast, God's order, administered by the Spirit, is concerned for the welfare of all without exception.

The debate among the Pharisees is inconclusive. So they go to the former blind man with the question: "What do you say about him?" (9:17). His response is prompt and revealing:

"He is a prophet" (9:17). This represents a significant advance in his relationship to Jesus. After reflection, he is now prepared to declare his personal conviction that Jesus is a man of God, one who comes from God and speaks for God. He no longer needs to depend on the witness of others. Thus, he represents a stage of mature faith, which should be the normal development from childhood to early adulthood. In a modern social situation, this stage is often reached when young adults leave home to attend college. Their faith must now become more mature and personal for it will never survive if it is still little more than the "borrowed" faith of their parents.

"He is of age; ask him" (9:23)

It is surprising that so much attention is given to the parents of the former blind man. On one level, it seems to be simply a desperate attempt on the part of the Pharisees to find a way out of their dilemma. Perhaps the parents will be able to suggest something that they have overlooked. On another level, however, this seems to be the author's way of making certain that we do not miss the point that the former blind man has indeed progressed to a new and more personal relationship with Jesus. When they say, in verses 21 and 23, that their son is of age and should be allowed to speak for himself, they are clearly indicating that he has indeed moved out of the family circle and is an adult who can make adult decisions. This separation from family influence involves a risk, but it is the only way to achieve a personal identity that will make possible the mystical union with God that is the ideal of the community of John.

It may be worth noting also that this passage is a clear example of the kind of interweaving that the author uses in blending the experience of Jesus and that of the Johannine community. There is absolutely no other evidence that the followers of Jesus were being threatened with expulsion from the synagogue during the historical ministry of Jesus in the late 20s. On the contrary, we see in Luke 4:16-21 that Jesus himself was made welcome in a synagogue and was asked to take one of the readings. On the other hand, there is ample evidence of animosity between the members of the community of John and their Jewish compatriots in the late first century. As mentioned earlier, this tolerance of anachronism is probably due to the mystical tendencies of the Johannine community, which caused them to identify with Jesus to the point of telescoping, as it were, the historical periods that separated them from him.

"You are his disciple, but we are disciples of Moses" (9:28)

Finally, the Pharisees call the former blind man once again and foolishly urge him to do the impossible, that is, to deny that he has been cured by Jesus. The former blind man marvels at their persistence and wonders (perhaps not so naively) whether they might wish themselves to become disciples of Jesus. The reaction is predictable: "Then they reviled him, saying, 'You are his disciple, but we are disciples of Moses. We know that God has spoken to Moses, but as for this man, we do not know where he comes from'" (9:28-29). How sad to see them appeal to the familiar past in order to escape from the challenge of the present and the future! This stratagem is exactly the same one that we saw in John 8, except that there it was an appeal to Abraham.

It is evident now that the primary charge that the Johannine community levels against their Jewish antagonists is that they are stuck in the past. It is admirable indeed to honor the memory of ancestors, but too often that means only that one invokes their names to justify a tradition that has become something that these ancestors would never recognize. Over the centuries the Law of Moses has been edited and "massaged" to the point that it is no longer a challenge to selfish control and power politics. Jesus makes this charge quite explicit in the Gospel of Mark: You are "thus making void the word of God through your tradition . . ." (7:13). Thus, the heavily edited and familiar past is preferred to the unknown and uncontrollable future. This might have been excusable if Jesus had not come and offered a future that is full of light and glory, but which also requires profound personal conversion.

The former blind man, who is not at all beholden to the past, sees this with perfect clarity: "The man answered, 'Here is an astonishing thing! You do not know where he comes from, and yet he opened my eyes'" (9:30). One can only marvel at the extent to which the obvious is denied in order to protect a position that is familiar and controllable.

Raymond Brown has pointed out that, just as the blind man grows toward better vision and brighter light, so also the Pharisees are sinking into worse blindness and deeper darkness. He writes: "While the former blind man is gradually having his eyes opened to the truth about Jesus, the Pharisees or 'the Jews' are becoming more obdurate in their failure to see the truth" (*The Gospel according to John*, vol. 1, 377). Of course, this is not just about some people who lived at the end of the first century and had trouble with new teachings. It is about anyone in any age who rejects a teaching just because it is unfamiliar or because it challenges old prejudices, and it is always a tragedy when the future is sacrificed in defense of a past that is dead and gone.

"Do you believe in the Son of Man?" (9:35)

Jesus seeks out the former blind man. He has received his physical sight, but that is only the beginning of the miracle. Jesus wants him to see in a spiritual way also. He asks him, therefore: "Do you believe in the Son of Man?" (9:35). The term "son of man" was a title that Jesus often used in the Synoptic Gospels in reference to himself. It is an ambiguous title for it can mean simply a human being, or it can also have subtle messianic implications because of the text in the book of Daniel: "and behold, with the clouds of heaven / there came one like a son of man . . ." (7:13, RSV). Jesus seems to have used this ambiguous identification to discourage political interpretations of his mission.

Such a title means nothing to the former blind man and so he asks: "And who is he, sir? Tell me, so that I may believe in him" (9:36). The former blind man is more than ready to believe in Jesus as a person, but he is confused by the title that Jesus uses. I think that this is John's way of reminding us that titles, like rituals, can be useful at times but that they are only meant to lead us to something deeper, which is a personal, mystical union with God. The former blind man is, therefore, a model for all of us. He believes in the person of Jesus, not in some title, however appropriate, that may be used in reference to him.

Jesus waves away the title, therefore, and says to him: "You have seen him, and the one speaking with you is he" (9:37). The words, "You have seen him," have boundless implications. They mean that he can now see Jesus with more than his physical eyes; he can now see in a whole new, spiritual way. He is now truly enlightened. It is only now, therefore, that the miracle is complete, and with this new vision, the former blind man can cry out, "Lord, I believe" (9:38). He has come a long way from the time when he knew the Lord only as "the man called Jesus" (9:11), or even as "a prophet" (9:17).

It is clear that John wants all Christians to make that same journey: from childhood, when Jesus is accepted through the witness of believing parents, to early adulthood, when Jesus is accepted with personal faith but still mainly through titles, to Christian maturity, when Jesus has become an inseparable friend and the center of one's life. It is only in this final stage that we can claim to be truly enlightened as we begin to see things as they really are. For it is only in this final stage that we can know that truth about our human existence that Jesus came to reveal.

"I came into this world for judgment" (9:39)

John cannot leave this subject of enlightenment without reminding us once again that the revelation of Jesus demands a decision and results in a judgment. "I came into this world for judgment so that those who do not see may see, and those who do see may become blind" (9:39). The Pharisees know that he is referring to them, and so they protest: "Surely we are not blind, are we?" (9:40). The response of Jesus is chilling: "If you were blind, you would not have sin. But now that you say, 'We see,' your sin remains" (9:41). If they had not seen Jesus and witnessed his miracle, they could perhaps claim inculpable ignorance. But they have preferred their human understanding to his divine revelation and their doom is sealed.

In reading this passage, the one mistake that we must avoid at all cost is the conclusion that this warning pertains only to some Pharisees many years ago. It is so tempting to cling to a concept of religion that is so familiar and comprehensible that it leaves no room for the mystery of God. When we succumb to this temptation it is always a tragedy because it means that we will never see the glory that is at the center of that Mystery. On the other hand, when we understand that theology and biblical studies and rituals and titles are all intended to lead us safely to that wonderful center of Mystery, then we will begin to be truly enlightened. For then we will be able to join the former blind man and say with him: "Lord, I believe" (9:38). We will also follow his example as we worship. All authentic biblical studies thus lead quite naturally to praise and contemplation.

12

Eternal Life

Enlightenment is the sign of a mature faith but it is not an end in itself. In John's Gospel, the whole purpose of the coming of Jesus is that we may know the truth and that, in living it, we may come to fullness of life. The final words of chapter 20 leave no doubt on this score:

> Now Jesus did many other signs in the presence of his disciples, which are not written in this book. But these are written so that you may come to believe that Jesus is the Messiah, the Son of God, *and that through believing you may have life in his name* (20:30-31, emphasis added).

This is far more than physical life, of course. Indeed, John often refers to it as "eternal life" (e.g., 3:15-16). For it is a mystical union with the author of life and is, therefore, completely impervious to sickness or death. In fact, it is synonymous with ultimate freedom, which is also a result of knowing the truth: "you will know the truth, and the truth will make you free" (8:32).

L. William Countryman is surely right, once again, when he maintains that, in John's Gospel, the final step in the process that began with conversion is this fullness of life (*The Mystical Way in the Fourth Gospel,* 2nd ed., 77). This process from initial conversion to full mystical communion would be, therefore, the inner logic that governs the development of the first half of the Gospel. It is fairly obvious that the story of the raising of Lazarus from death to life in chapter 11 pertains to the theme of life. But Countryman believes that this theme embraces chapter 10 also where Jesus is presented as the Good Shepherd who protects and nourishes the lives of his sheep by giving his own life for them.

"He calls his own sheep by name and leads them out" (10:3)

The imagery used in this parable presupposes a personal knowledge of sheep herding in the ancient world. During the rainy winter season, the sheep remained in one place where grass was plentiful, and at night they were herded into a corral where they would be safe from wild animals. Jesus calls those who would enter this safe haven for mischief marauders, thieves, and bandits (10:1). In terms of the parable, they mislead Israel since they have no mandate from God. This group would include the Pharisees and Sadducees, as well as other misguided leaders.

Jesus, being the true shepherd, enters the sheepfold by the door. He calls the sheep by name, just as traditional shepherds used a distinctive call or whistle to summon their sheep. All human hearts are made to respond to God's call. This sensitivity is natural and instinctive, not unlike the experience of one who has the gift of perfect pitch. However, this sensitivity to God's voice can easily be lost if one takes refuge behind layers of fear and distrust. Jesus speaks gently to us as he tries to reassure those who have suffered violence. His sole interest is love and care; he does not seek power or domination. "When he has brought out all his own, he goes ahead of them, and the sheep follow him because they know his voice" (10:4). When we allow his call to touch our hearts, he leads us out to pasture—to the nourishment that gives eternal life.

"I am the good shepherd" (10:11)

Those of us who are not personally acquainted with sheep herding can easily be misled by romantic notions here. Countryman notes:

> In Greek and Latin literature of the Hellenistic Age, the imagery generally evoked an idealized, uncomplicated country life as portrayed in pastoral poetry. . . . It is more likely that the shepherd imagery here is royal imagery. "Shepherd" was the common synonym for "ruler" in the Jewish scriptures. . . . That is the meaning, for example, in "The Lord is my shepherd" . . . (*The Mystical Way in the Fourth Gospel,* 2nd ed., 78).

This is in keeping with the general biblical image of kingship, which is viewed as beneficent and protective rather than domineering and exploitative.

When Jesus says that he is the Good Shepherd we must not entertain images of some idyllic pastoral situation. Sheep herding was hard work and sometimes required the exposure of one's life to danger or death. When Jesus says, therefore, "The good shepherd lays down his life for the sheep" (10:11), he is not using hyperbole. In fact, it is this readiness to give his life for the sheep that separates the good shepherd from the hireling who has no personal or emotional concern for his sheep. For him, it is a job, not a vocation. He is interested in the sheep but he does not love them. "The hired hand runs away because a hired hand does not care for the sheep" (10:13). By contrast, Jesus is prepared to sacrifice his very life for the sheep in his care: "I lay down my life for the sheep" (10:15). He gives his life for us who have been committed to his loving care.

"I know my own and my own know me" (10:14)

When we apply this parable to our human situation, it is clear that the relationship between Jesus and ourselves is not at all the kind of blind loyalty that characterizes sheep in reference to their shepherds. Rather, we are united with Jesus through a personal, mystical bond that is similar to that which exists between Jesus and his heavenly Father. "I know my own and my own know me, just as the Father knows me and I know the Father" (10:14-15). This is a truly amazing statement and its implications defy full comprehension. The generous believer is drawn into the flow of life that courses between the persons of the Trinity. This represents the fullness of life, compared to which our everyday life is scarcely more than sleepwalking.

Since Jesus is a good and loving shepherd, his concern reaches out to all the sheep, wherever they may be. "I have other sheep that do not belong to this fold. I must bring them also, and they will listen to my voice. So there will be one flock, one shepherd" (10:16). The kind of love that animates Jesus, and should animate his followers, can never be satisfied with merely receiving the gift of life. It must constantly reach out to others so that they too may share in this ultimate gift. And this union of life will overcome all the negative and divisive forces that lead to death. These words take on special significance for those who are rightly distressed by the disunity that exists between Christians. And the principle seems to be clear: Do not be so concerned about diversity; be concerned rather about the lack of love.

"I have told you, and you do not believe" (10:25)

Jesus creates a real dilemma for those who hear him. They are attracted to him, but they are held back by their preconceived notions about the Messiah. He talks about laying down his life in obedience to his Father; they are looking for a leader who will liberate their country from the Romans. They know that he has power but they cannot understand why he will not use his power for their purposes. "How long will you keep us in suspense? If you are the Messiah, tell us plainly" (10:24). The problem is that he has been telling them that plainly but they cannot hear him because they are wedded to their own ideas and to their personal agendas.

They need to clear the slate so that Jesus can write his message on it. "I have told you, and you do not believe. The works that I do in my Father's name testify to me; but you do not believe, because you do not belong to my sheep" (10:25-26). This does not mean that they are fated or predestined to be closed to the message of Jesus. If they do not belong to the flock of Jesus, it is because they choose not to be converted from old habits and prejudices. When we meet people today who have racist tendencies, we know how difficult it is for them to abandon stereotypes. It was this kind of religious prejudice that kept people from trusting Jesus. His deeds were good, but he was just too different. Why couldn't he be good without asking them to change? We can almost hear Jesus' reply: Why can't you trust your instincts and let go of old familiar ways which are outmoded because they prevent the realization of God's loving purposes?

"I give them eternal life, and they will never perish" (10:28)

Those who are willing to let go of the false security of old, familiar ways will come to recognize and to trust the call of Jesus: "My sheep hear my voice. I know them, and they follow me" (10:27). To draw another analogy from sheep herding, the ewe will not accept a lamb that does not have her scent, but she will suckle and protect the one that does. Jesus wants to nourish and protect us, but we must first be willing to trust his message of unselfish love. The grace to do so is always there; we must not be afraid to cooperate with it.

It does not appear that unselfish loving will benefit us. However, the more we adopt this way of living, the more we will begin to share in the life that Jesus offers us. His words are immensely encouraging: "I give them eternal life, and they will never perish" (10:28). Moreover, we will find that the old security that we thought might be adequate will be replaced with the only security that has any validity. "No one will snatch them out of my hand" (10:28). This is so because the Father has entrusted us to Jesus who will fiercely defend us against all possible hurt. The love of the Father and the love of Jesus are equally protective. In this respect also, "The Father and I are one" (10:30).

When one offers far more than is expected, the consequence is usually either joy or anger. Unfortunately, Jesus' claim
to be one with the heavenly Father is greeted with anger: "The
Jews took up stones again to stone him" (10:31). This was the
standard response to perceived blasphemy. For they are certain
that Jesus is claiming too much for himself when he says that
he is one with the Father. In fact, however, he is claiming too
much for them. For he is inviting them to participate in his divinity, as he suggests by referring to Psalm 82:6: "I say, You are
gods, children of the of the Most High, all of you" (10:34).

In effect, Jesus is pleading with them to trust their experience rather than old religious structures: "If I am not doing
the works of my Father, then do not believe me. But if I do
them, even though you do not believe me, believe the works,
so that you may know and understand that the Father is in me
and I am in the Father" (10:37-38). But it is all to no avail.
"Then they tried to arrest him again . . ." (10:39).

The resistance that Jesus experiences is also the resistance
that the community of John found when they talked about the
mystical union to which God calls us. The Johannine community is convinced that God is calling us all to a union with him,
in Jesus, which is far deeper and more personal than we can
imagine. Through the words of Jesus, the community expresses
its frustration that their contemporaries are so unwilling to embrace that blessed possibility of eternal life for us mere mortals.

"Now a certain man was ill, Lazarus of Bethany" (11:1)

Jesus has promised eternal life to those who hear and follow him (10:28). In raising Lazarus from the dead, he now
provides an example of his power to give life. There is something curious about the opening sentence. One would expect
the author to name Lazarus first and then tell us that he was
ill. In fact, some translators have "corrected" John's awkward
phrasing. But this is probably exactly what John meant to say,
for the story is not just about a certain Lazarus who lived many
centuries ago. It is about "Everyman," since all human beings

are ill with the incurable disease of mortality. Lazarus simply represents all of us as we come to Jesus to seek healing and life.

John tells us that Lazarus was from Bethany, "the village of Mary and her sister Martha" (11:1). Bethany was a village situated just over the crest of the Mount of Olives to the east of Jerusalem. Jesus seems to have stayed there with his friends when he visited Jerusalem. A perceptive reader will notice something unusual about the way Mary and Martha are introduced. For Mary is named first and Martha is mentioned only as "her sister." This alerts us to the roles that these two sisters of Lazarus will play in the story that follows. Martha will have the first opportunity to speak with Jesus, but Mary will have the favored role and will be the one who causes Jesus to confront death and conquer it. In fact, one almost feels sorry for Lazarus, who is the subject of the story, yet spends most of his time in the grave and, when finally released, is not given a single word to say. This tells us that the story is not just about three friends of Jesus, but carries profound symbolic implications that affect all of us.

"Lord, he whom you love is ill" (11:3)

In 10:40, Jesus is said to have gone "across the Jordan" where he presumably was when word was brought to him about the illness of his friend Lazarus. Once again, one would expect a more personal and specific identification than the rather vague "he whom you love." They surely would have known that Lazarus was not the only person whom Jesus loved. But the language used reminds us once again that this story must be read on two levels. It is about a man named Lazarus who was a friend of Jesus, but it is also about each of us who must sooner or later cope with the universal human fate of death. It is very consoling to see, then, that we too can be identified as those whom Jesus loves.

In fact, one notes that in this story there is a kind of regular refrain that reminds us of the love that existed between Jesus and his friends. Illness and death are thus opposed by the even greater power of love. In spite of his love for Lazarus and his sisters, which is reasserted in verse 5, and in spite of the urgency of the request, Jesus does not respond for two days. At a deeper level, this alerts us to the fact that the raising of Lazarus is a preview of the resurrection of Jesus himself, which took place two days after his crucifixion.

"Are there not twelve hours of daylight?" (11:9)

When Jesus finally decides to go to Judea, where his friends are living, his disciples protest that this is a dangerous place for him: "Rabbi, the Jews were just now trying to stone you, and are you going there again?" (11:8). The response of Jesus is enigmatic, to say the least. "Are there not twelve hours of daylight? Those who walk during the day do not stumble, because they see the light of this world. But those who walk at night stumble, because the light is not in them" (11:9-10). Although it is true that people rarely stumble when they can see where they are going, it is clear that Jesus has a different kind of light in mind.

Jesus himself is "the light of the world" (8:12), in the sense that he has given us the revelation that illuminates the purpose of our existence. Those who accept this truth, and live its message of unselfish love, will be able to walk safely toward that heavenly homeland which is the culmination of life as God intends it. What Jesus is telling his disciples, therefore, is that his going to Judea, though clearly dangerous from a merely human perspective, is an act of love and is therefore safer in the long run than ignoring the need of his friend.

Most of us have probably noticed that an appeal for help often comes at an inconvenient time and sometimes calls us to an unhealthy or dangerous place. Human prudence may counsel us to play it safe, but this could very well mean "walking in the darkness" and stumbling. This going to a dangerous place for the sake of Lazarus is also a preview of Jesus' going to Judea to meet the ultimate danger of crucifixion—and, beyond that, glorious victory. Loving others, therefore, can be a dangerous undertaking, but it is the only safe way to live.

"Martha . . . went and met him, while Mary stayed at home" (11:20)

When Jesus arrives at Bethany, he discovers that his friend Lazarus has died and has "already been in the tomb four days" (11:17). This information is meant to underline the reality of his death. The mourners have gathered to console the two bereaved sisters. Even before Jesus enters the village, word comes that he is approaching. Martha hurries out to meet him, while Mary stays at home. This contrasting reaction of the two sisters is a kind of body language that reveals their contrasting roles in the drama of the raising of Lazarus. In fact, they represent two ways of responding to the trauma of death in human experience.

Martha is impatient. She wants to wrestle with the terrible scandal of death among humans who yearn for immortality. She has a thousand ways of saying, "Why?" She is frustrated that Jesus could not have come sooner: "Lord, if you had been here, my brother would not have died" (11:21). She knows that Jesus loves Lazarus and has worked miracles of healing. Why could he not have done the same for his friend? Thus, she represents all of us who struggle to understand death, who shake it furiously, like a little dog with a rag doll, to find the meaning of it. We can easily empathize with Martha in her impatience and frustration.

"I am the resurrection and the life" (11:25)

Jesus responds to the grief of Martha with the consoling words, "Your brother will rise again" (11:23). Martha takes this to be a kind of funeral parlor cliché, for she says. "I know that he will rise again in the resurrection on the last day" (11:24). She was hoping for something much more immediate than that, however. Jesus then counters with a statement that has been recognized as one of the most profound assertions in John's Gospel: "I am the resurrection and the life" (11:25). These words have limitless implications, for they imply that resurrection and life are inseparable from Jesus and that all who remain attached to him cannot fail to participate in them. To be one with Jesus is to be part of life.

Jesus continues with words that explain more fully how he represents resurrection and life in our situation of sickness and death: "Those who believe in me, even though they die, will live, and everyone who lives and believes in me will never die" (11:25-26). There is a kind of progression in this statement. In the first stage, Jesus declares that all those who believe in him and live in accordance with his teaching of loving service, even though they die like all other mortals, will be rescued from death and will share in his resurrection. In fact, because of their willingness to respond to the need of others, they may even die sooner than if they made safety a first priority.

The second part of the statement is more absolute: those who live and believe in Jesus, by participating in his love for others, will never have to die. In other words, though they will indeed expire, it will be a death that is no more than a final opportunity to love and trust as they give themselves for others in obedience to God's will. It will not be what most would call an experience of dying. For these fortunate ones, death will be just another way of loving.

For a community that places a high premium on mystical union with God, this experience of living on a level that is impervious to the ravages of death is proof positive that they have responded perfectly to the coming of Jesus into our world. Indeed, truly believing in Jesus, and therefore living in him, means also living in God, i.e., living in that flow of life that Jesus shares with his Father. This makes all other kinds of living seem unreal. Moreover, it drives out all the terrible experiences of fear, anxiety, and doubt as one sees only the illuminated horizon where the promises of a loving God will be realized. It is doubtful that the members of the Johannine community experienced this as an everyday occurrence. However, just an occasional glimpse of this transforming reality would suffice to fill one's life with hope and joy. No wonder they were so eager to share this discovery with their Jewish friends and with other Christian communities.

Unfortunately, Martha is not yet ready to receive this kind of revelation. When Jesus asks her, "Do you believe this?" she gives an answer that is a classic example of saying too much. "She said to him, 'Yes, Lord, I believe that you are the Messiah, the Son of God, the one coming into the world'" (11:27). A more appropriate answer would have been a simple, "Yes."

Raymond Brown writes:

> Throughout the incident involving Martha we see that she believes in Jesus but inadequately. In vs. 27 she addresses him with lofty titles, probably the same titles used in the early Christian professions of faith; yet vs. 39 shows that she does not as yet believe in his power to give life (*The Gospel according to John*, vol. 1, 433).

In verse 39 Martha protests that they should not roll away the stone over the mouth of Lazarus' tomb because there will be a foul odor. Obviously, she cannot believe that Jesus has power over death if she thinks that he cannot deal even with the odor of death.

The answer of Martha to Jesus' question has other implications as well. It sounds like a memorized answer, such as a child might give in a catechism class. It is also an answer that is composed of titles, and we have already seen that John's community is very suspicious of theological titles which, like external rituals, may give an appearance of faith in Christ without a deep, personal union with him. Martha would represent therefore those Christians, of all times and places, who place a high premium on appearances of piety and on theological expertise without the mystical union with God which rituals and titles are meant to serve. This is, of course, no reflection on the historical Martha, but it does allow us to understand the symbolic role that she is asked to play. This becomes even clearer when we consider the reaction of her sister, Mary, to the presence of Jesus.

"*The Teacher is here and is calling for you*" (11:28)

While Martha rushes out to meet Jesus, her sister Mary remains at home. This does not mean that she is disinterested.

Rather, her attitude suggests that there is another way to deal with death. She accepts the fact of death in the quiet confidence that God will set things right in due time. She awaits God's initiative since she realizes that life and death have always been the province of God. We are told that Martha spoke to her "privately" or "quietly." There is something about Mary that makes everyone quiet down. She evokes a sense of contemplation; being near to her is like being in a holy place.

When Jesus calls Mary, she is quick to respond. She, like Martha, tells Jesus that he surely could have saved their brother if he had only arrived sooner. But the circumstances make her question more a prayer than a protest. The reaction of Jesus is much different too. "When Jesus saw her weeping . . . he was greatly disturbed in spirit and deeply moved" (11:33). In response to Martha's plea, Jesus offers a profound theological statement about resurrection—a wonderful reaction but still rather impersonal. When he hears Mary make the same plea, however, he reacts with strong personal and emotional involvement. The verbs here are much stronger than the English translation conveys. They suggest a mixture of grief and anger because of what death has done to the friends of Jesus.

It is very tempting to see, in this contrast between Martha and Mary, the difference that the author of the Gospel sees between the community of John and the other Christian communities. These other communities are notable for their clear doctrine, ritual correctness, and ecclesiastical structure. But they have not yet achieved the mystical awareness that characterizes the Johannine community. Martha would represent them because she knows all the proper titles of Jesus (11:27), but she has not yet reached the mystical and contemplative relationship with Jesus that Mary enjoys. Mary would represent the Johannine community with their deeper appreciation of a mystical relationship with Jesus—a relationship that impels Jesus to personal intervention in favor of Lazarus rather than simply issuing a doctrinal statement about resurrection. Both effects are good, but it is only intervention that guarantees life.

This then would be another example of the contrast that Raymond Brown has pointed out in the relationship in the Gospel between Peter and the Beloved Disciple, as we have noted in chapter 4 of this book. From this perspective, Mary, the mystical one, represents the community of the Beloved Disciple whereas Martha, with her knowledge of titles, represents the other Christian churches whose model is Peter. According to Brown's reconstruction of events, the community was wracked by division after the death of the Beloved Disciple, as reflected in the letters of John. It is then that they came to appreciate the value of a sober theology and good order in the Church. As many of their members went into schism, a chastened minority accepted the structure and safety of the broader Christian tradition, bringing with them the precious gift of their mystical sensitivity (cf. Raymond Brown, *The Community of the Beloved Disciple*, 146–7). Once again, it is the ancient biblical conviction that both king and prophet are needed in a healthy community of believers.

One may easily conclude from all this that the Johannine community was an elitist group in the early Church. A more balanced conclusion would be that offered by Raymond Brown who summarizes the situation when he writes:

> There is no clear evidence that the Johannine community was condemning apostolic foundation and succession, church offices, or church sacramental practices. The Fourth Gospel is best interpreted as voicing a warning against the dangers inherent in such developments by stressing what (for John) is truly essential, namely, the living presence of Jesus in the Christian through the Paraclete (*The Community of the Beloved Disciple*, 88).

In our present context, Martha (representing other Christian churches) is good, but Mary (representing the Johannine community) is better. What we need, of course, is both Martha and Mary. The sad tendency is to settle for correct "Martha" and neglect mystical "Mary." The entire Gospel of John, in my estimation, is a plea to restore Mary to her proper place in the Christian community.

"Unbind him, and let him go" (11:44)

Jesus, deeply moved by the plea and the tears of Mary, asks where they have buried Lazarus. He is now prepared to confront death, which has caused so much pain among those whom he loves. They respond, "Lord, come and see" (11:34), thus echoing the words of Jesus in 1:39, when he invited the disciples to "come and see," not death but life. With our unenlightened eyes, we can see only the cemetery, but Jesus asks us to follow him and find a life that cannot be touched by the cold hand of death.

At this point Jesus does something that is so out of character for the Jesus of John's Gospel that it is astonishing: "Jesus began to weep" (11:35). In the Fourth Gospel, Jesus is always in charge and seems to be above the fray. This exceptional behavior is, therefore, another example of the deeply personal and emotional side of Jesus that is evoked by the personal relationship that exists between him and Mary, the mystical and contemplative one.

Jesus then proceeds to the tomb and, when the stone is removed, cries out in a loud voice, "Lazarus, come out!" (11:43). Lazarus does emerge from his tomb, but there is something unusual about his appearance: "The dead man came out, his hands and feet bound with strips of cloth, and his face wrapped in a cloth" (11:44). This special condition of Lazarus is evidently intended to remind us that the raising of Lazarus, though a kind of preview of the resurrection of Jesus, is far inferior to that event because Jesus leaves the funeral wrappings behind and emerges from the tomb in total freedom (20:6-7). Jesus then commands: "Unbind him, and let him go" (11:44). These words of Jesus are an echo of the dramatic words of Moses: "Thus says the Lord, the God of Israel: 'Let my people go . . .'" (Exod 5:1). And, then as now, the message is the same: God wants us to be free—free from all kinds of bondage, including death, so that we may enjoy that fullness of eternal life that he has always intended for his beloved children.

Conclusion

"It is God the only Son . . . who has made him known" (1:18)

It may seem strange to present the Prologue of John's Gospel as a conclusion, but this is only because many assume too readily that it serves only as an introduction to the Gospel. In fact, it is more a résumé or summary than an introduction. Raymond Brown captures the sense of it when he describes the Prologue as a sketch of the career of the divine Word, beginning in eternity, carrying out his mission on earth, and then returning to the bosom of the heavenly Father. He expresses this in terms of a "pendulum swing" which comprehends the entire journey of the eternal Word, who became flesh among us, and then opened heaven so that we could return with him to the world of eternal life (*The Gospel according to John*, vol. 2, 541–2). For John, then, the story of Jesus begins, long before Bethlehem, in the realm of timeless eternity. It is there that the divine Word experienced the love of God, and it is from there that this Word came to our created world to tell us about God's love for us. Jesus, Word made flesh, "is God the only Son . . . who has made him known" (1:18).

"He was in the beginning with God" (1:2)

Most would agree that the Prologue is a very carefully constructed literary unit with recognizable elements. The first two verses are concerned with the relationship between the Word and God. The Word is said to have existed already when time began. The sense is captured when we note that the Greek is better translated, "In the beginning, the Word already was" (1:1). Thus, this Word is as old, or as young, as God himself. This eternal Word was, therefore, "with God," which clearly suggests a distinction between them. But there is no separation, for the text continues, "and the Word was God" (1:1).

Who is this mysterious Word, who is one with God, yet somehow distinct from him? Perhaps the best way to picture this phenomenon is to say that the Word is, in a sense, God speaking himself, or God reaching out, seeking to share and to love. The Canadian philosopher Leslie Dewart has noted that a word is "the extension of a person into his environment" (*Religion, Language and Truth*, 45). This may be as close as we can come to conveying John's sublime concept in our inadequate human language. In fact, throughout the Gospel of John, as we have seen, Jesus is presented as the one in whom the Father reveals to us his hidden nature as One who loves. The God that Jesus reveals is a loving parent who wishes to embrace rather than strike.

From this it follows that, when John calls Jesus the Word of God, he does not intend to tell us about Jesus' nature as a Person of the Trinity. Rather, he is concerned only with the function or mission of Jesus. Just as a human word reveals a hidden thought, so Jesus' mission is to reveal to us the hidden nature of God. John knows this, not through theological reasoning, but through personal experience. What he experiences is God's overwhelming love. We are tempted to believe that God is only powerful, and this frightens us, but Jesus tells us that he is, by personal preference, loving and caring and forgiving. This does not mean that we cannot persist in sin and thus destroy ourselves, but that is the last thing God wants to see happen.

This understanding of "word" is deeply rooted in the Hebrew Scriptures, and there is no need to look for its meaning in the various Greek philosophies of John's day. As Alexander Jones has pointed out, the initial divine word was the *fiat,* or "let there be," of the original creation, followed by the "words" of the Law, and the Prophets and the Wisdom writings. Finally, the story of this divine communication ends with the arrival in our world of the perfect and ultimate Word, who is Jesus ("The Word Is a Seed" in *The Bridge,* vol. 2, 13–34). This final incarnation of God's message is spoken primarily to our hearts. We need to study it endlessly but, most of all, we need to meet it and welcome it into the center of our being. John can never be satisfied with less than a mystical union with this Jesus who is the incarnation of divine love.

"All things came into being through him" (1:3)

After considering the relationship between the Word and God, John now turns his attention to the special relationship between the Word and creation. Since the Word is an eternal manifestation of God's reaching out in love, it follows that the created universe is simply a further expression of that same love. One way of seeing this is to imagine that the light of God's love is refracted through the prism of the Word to form a million colorful rays of light that touch every creature in the universe. Thus, even the tiniest element of creation speaks of God's love. Moreover, since in Hebrew thought creation is a continuous activity of God, all creation, at all times, represents and constantly reminds us of the reality and presence of God. We live in that presence as a fish lives in the sea. To a person of mystical sensitivity, all of creation proclaims, therefore, the reality of the presence and love of God. To develop one's mystical nature means to become sensitized to that all-pervasive presence of God among us—a presence that is more real than anything that we can touch or see.

Since creation continues to flow, as it were, from the fingertips of God, it is not surprising that John sees the primary qualities of creation to be life and light. "What has come into being in him was life, and the life was the light of all people" (1:4). Thus, the first thing one notes about this creation is its vitality. Creation, as God plans it, is dancing with life. It is, as Jesus told the Samaritan woman (4:14), like a spring of fresh water, bubbling up and inexhaustible. Death as we know it is not part of God's plan. God created the world in "mint condition"; if it has become tarnished, that is a later development.

This pristine creation is also full of light. In the ancient world, light had profound symbolic meaning. It was so much more than mere illumination. Since they did not have artificial light, they associated warmth and fertility with the light of the sun. Moreover, since one cannot see a path in the dark, light represented meaning and purpose and security in life. As we have noted, the author of Genesis considered light to be the first work of creation, because that was the first discovery of the Hebrew slaves when God delivered them from bondage. By liberating them, God gave them a future and showed them a way. Thus, the meaning of human existence was never meant to be a riddle. From God's perspective, it is all very clear. It is human sinfulness that has obscured the picture.

This fact of human sinfulness is noted almost immediately: "The light shines in the darkness, and the darkness did not overcome it" (1:5). John does not speculate about the origin of this darkness but we know that it came from a misuse of the wonderful gift of freedom. Nonetheless, there has never really been any doubt about the victory of the light over this darkness. From John's perspective, we are challenged to use our freedom to reverse the effects of that sinfulness by choosing to live unselfishly. This is exactly what Jesus did, and he has come to help us to become part of that loving which dispels the darkness and leads to true life.

"There was a man sent from God, whose name was John" (1:6)

The author's specific reference to John the Baptist is surprising in a context where he has thus far painted with broad brush strokes. But the final editor of the Gospel certainly considered this apparent interruption appropriate and that means that we should listen carefully to its message. The emphasis is on witnessing, and the implication is that it will be almost impossible for us to choose the light without the service of witnesses. John stresses the importance of a personal union with Jesus, but this does not mean that he minimizes the significance of community, and it is only in community that one can benefit from the service of witnessing. God can come to us in many ways, of course, but the normal way is through other people. This makes good sense when we realize that paying attention to others is part of that unselfishness which is the essence of our communion with God.

John the Baptist showed that unselfish concern for others and this impelled him to bear witness to the discovery that he had made. "He came as a witness to testify to the light, so that all might believe through him" (1:7). The sole purpose of the Baptist was, therefore, to enable others to see the light that had been revealed to him. Entertaining the divine light is not a private affair. It requires the help of others, for which we must be grateful, and it demands that we share it with others. Thus, apostolic and missionary mandates are not optional for one who has seen the light.

"But to all who received him . . . he gave power to become children of God" (1:12)

After the brief reference to John the Baptist, we return again to the career of the eternal Word and we are told that he came into a world where he was not generally welcomed. "He came to what was his own, and his own people did not accept him" (1:11). This third stage in the career of the divine Word represents his presence, not only in creation generally but specifically in human history. There is a disagreement among commentators about the meaning of this verse. The traditional view has been that, when John says that the Word "came to what was his own," he is referring to the presence of the Word in the period before Christ, i.e., in the "journey" from creation, through the Law and Prophets and Wisdom writings. The coming of the Word in the person of Jesus would then be first mentioned in verse 14: "And the Word became flesh. . . ."

Raymond Brown argues persuasively, however, that the coming of the eternal Word in the person of Jesus is intended already in verse 11. His argument is based upon the *effect* of this coming "to what was his own," namely, the possibility of becoming children of God (1:12). He points out that becoming a child of God, as described in Jesus' dialogue with Nicodemus in chapter 3, requires that one be born from above through a baptism in the Spirit—something that is possible only *after* the coming of Jesus (see *The Gospel according to John*, vol. 1, 29). Thus, when we are told that the divine Word was not accepted by his own people, it means that Jesus, now the Word made flesh, was not welcomed by most of those whom he encountered in the Israel of his day. This is probably also a reflection of the experience of the Johannine community at the end of the first century who found it so difficult to understand why Jesus was not accepted by so many of their friends and neighbors.

John is quick to remind us, however, that though many did not accept Jesus there were some few who did accept him and believed in him. These trusted his words and changed their lives in accordance with his message. The incredible result was that they became God's very own children, secure and serene in the sure knowledge of a divine parent's love for them, and therefore without anxiety about the future, since they are assured of the rich inheritance of God's kingdom. Moreover, just as children resemble their parents, so these also will be like God in their commitment to unselfish love in every facet of their lives.

"And the Word became flesh and lived among us" (1:14)

Since the incarnation of the Word in the person of Jesus has already been noted in verse 11, we should understand the first words of verse 14 as a recapitulation: And *so* the Word became flesh. . . . The emphasis then shifts from the fact of the divine incarnation to its *effects* in our world, and those effects are dramatic indeed. We note that John does not say that he "lived with me," but rather "among us." In fact, all the effects of the coming of Jesus are expressed in terms of the creation of a human *community* that would not be possible without Jesus.

The nature of this very special kind of community is revealed in the words that open 1 John:

> We declare to you what was from the beginning, what we have heard, what we have seen with our eyes, what we have looked at and touched with our hands, concerning the word of life—this life was revealed, and we have seen it and testify to it, and declare to you the eternal life that was with the Father and was revealed to us—we declare to you what we have seen and heard so that you also may have fellowship with us; and truly our fellowship is with the Father and with his Son Jesus Christ (1 John 1:1-3).

This is mystical language. But they are not just the words of an individual in union with God, but of members of a mystical community who have found their unity in their common bond with God and with one another in God. We should also note the experiential nature of this description, for when John says that they "looked at" this divine Word made flesh, it suggests a loving gaze, a contemplation. And when they "touched with their hands," it is as if they caressed Jesus, much as an unseeing person "reads" another's face with sensitive fingertips.

"And we have seen his glory, the glory as of a father's only son, full of grace and truth" (1:14)

When this mystical community, established by the love of God, looks upon Jesus, they see his "glory." The biblical concept of glory is quite different from our common understanding of it as a spectacular display of some sort. In the Bible the glory of God is simply a manifestation of God's presence in some way that we can understand. Thus, when John says that his community has seen the glory of Jesus, it means that they discover in him a perfect manifestation of the loving nature of the hidden God. That is why he goes on to declare that this glory is "the glory as of a father's only son." For, just as a child reproduces in some sense the nature of its parents, so Jesus represents faithfully the nature of his heavenly Father.

This only Son of the Father made present among us is said to be "full of grace and truth" (1:14). Raymond Brown has concluded that this phrase refers to those attributes of God which Israel loved to recall, namely, God's loving kindness and fidelity, which he translates as "enduring love" (*The Gospel according to John*, vol. 1, 14). In this interpretation, Jesus would be the perfect incarnation of these attributes in our world. This is a very attractive interpretation and it is certainly true whether or not that is the meaning of this text.

In my judgment, however, Ignace de la Potterie offers an interpretation that is more in keeping with the theology of John's Gospel as a whole. He maintains that the primary focus here is that *truth* which Jesus brings to us from the Father and which is the essence of his revelation. His would translate the passage, therefore, not "full of grace and truth," but "filled with the gift of truth." Jesus is the Father's gift to us and the essence of that gift is the truth or revelation that Jesus brings. In fact, he is himself the embodiment of that revelation (*La Vérité dans Saint Jean*, 240–1). This interpretation is also in perfect harmony with those decisive words of Jesus before Pilate: "For this I was born, and for this I came into the world, to testify to the truth" (18:37). Thus, the incarnation of Jesus is the manifestation of the ultimate *truth*, which is also the supreme *gift*, because it reveals that which is more important than anything that we could ever imagine, namely, God's unconditional love for us.

"It is God the only Son, who is close to the Father's heart, who has made him known" (1:18)

This gift of revelation that Jesus brings to us surpasses by far the wonderful revelation brought by Moses. "The Law indeed was given through Moses; the gift of truth came through Jesus Christ" (1:17, author's translation). The people of Israel always, and rightly, considered themselves blest to have received from God the revelation of the Torah, which enabled them to learn of God's purposes in this world. However, the length and breadth and depth of God's love for us became evident only in Jesus, whom the Father sent to die for us. "For God so loved the world that he gave his only Son . . ." (3:16). The revelation of God's love is no longer expressed in the words of Moses alone but is now made manifest in the very person of Jesus. The wonderful Torah is thus eclipsed by the even more wonderful Word of God made flesh.

John concludes his summary of the career of Jesus by noting the conviction of ancient Israel that it is impossible for any human being to see God. Even Moses, God's special friend, had to hide in the cave as the Lord passed by (Exod 33:18-23). But all that has now changed. For Jesus is the hidden God made visible to us. He is the very Son of God, "who is close to the Father's heart" (1:18), where he can hear the heartbeat of God and learn all his secrets. One can scarcely imagine an image that would convey more effectively the intimacy between Jesus and his heavenly Father. All through the Gospel of John, Jesus speaks of this unbreakable bond between him and his Father. He insists on this because his message of unselfish love is so difficult to accept that he wants us to know that he has received it directly from our Creator.

The whole purpose of the coming of Jesus into our world is, therefore, to make known the Father (1:18). We can say that, as a general rule, God has a "bad press." He is blamed for almost everything that we find hard to accept. Most of all, I think, he is blamed for making us fragile and mortal human beings. However, when we see his own Son taking on that fragility and mortality and making it an instrument of his loving, we should conclude that God's love can be victorious in our lives also. When the author of the Gospel of John, who is called the "one whom Jesus loved," reclines next to him at the

Last Supper (13:23), we are surely meant to conclude that he is close to the heart of Jesus, just as Jesus is close to the Father's heart. As such, he is able to speak to us most eloquently about the love of the Father that comes to us through his beloved Son.

This then is the *truth*, to which John's Gospel is devoted. We are called into being because God loves us. We are asked to open ourselves to every manifestation of love and goodness in our lives, so that we may become free and confident. Then, we are offered the wonderful opportunity to join Jesus in converting our precious freedom into loving service of others. This will be painful at times, but the outcome is an incredible victory as we participate in the glorious resurrection of Jesus and thus find our way back to the Father, who loves us beyond comprehension and who awaits us with open arms.

Bibliography

Brown, Raymond. *The Community of the Beloved Disciple.* New York: Paulist Press, 1979.

_____. *The Gospel according to John.* Anchor Bible. 2 vols. Garden City, N.Y.: Doubleday, 1966, 1970.

Countryman, L. William. *The Mystical Way in the Fourth Gospel.* 2nd ed. Valley Forge, Penn.: Trinity Press International, 1994.

Dewart, Leslie. *Religion, Language and Truth.* New York: Herder and Herder, 1970.

Dumm, Demetrius. *Flowers in the Desert.* New York: Paulist Press, 1987.

The Interpretation of the Bible in the Church. The Pontifical Biblical Commission. Washington, D.C.: United States Catholic Conference, 1993.

Jones, Alexander. "The Word Is a Seed." *The Bridge,* vol. 2. New York: Pantheon Books, 1956, 13–34.

The Oxford English Dictionary. London: Oxford University Press, 1971.

Potterie, Ignace de la. *La Vérité dans Saint Jean.* 2 vols. AnBib 73–4. Rome: Biblical Institute Press, 1977.

Schneiders, Sandra. *The Revelatory Text.* 2nd ed. Collegeville: The Liturgical Press, 1999.

_____. *Written That You May Believe.* A Herder and Herder Book. New York: Crossroads Publishing Co., 1999.
Underhill, Evelyn. *Practical Mysticism.* Columbus, Ohio: Ariel Press, 1986.

Index of Authors

Scripture Index